VW BUS

Forty years of Splitties, Bays & Wedges

Also from Veloce Publishing

Speedpro Series
Volkswagen Beetle Suspension, Brakes & Chassis, How to Modify For High Performance (Hale)
Volkswagen Bus Suspension, Brakes & Chassis for High Performance, How to Modify – Updated & Enlarged New Edition (Hale)

Enthusiast's Restoration Manual Series
Citroën 2CV, How to Restore (Porter)
Classic Car Bodywork, How to Restore (Thaddeus)
Classic British Car Electrical Systems (Astley)
Classic Car Electrics (Thaddeus)
Classic Cars, How to Paint (Thaddeus)
Jaguar E-type (Crespin)
Reliant Regal, How to Restore (Payne)
Triumph TR2, 3, 3A, 4 & 4A, How to Restore (Williams)
Triumph TR5/250 & 6, How to Restore (Williams)
Triumph TR7/8, How to Restore (Williams)
Triumph Trident T150/T160 & BSA Rocket III, How to Restore (Rooke)
Ultimate Mini Restoration Manual, The (Ayre & Webber)
Volkswagen Beetle, How to Restore (Tyler)
VW Bay Window Bus (Paxton)

Essential Buyer's Guide Series
VW Beetle (Cservenka & Copping)
VW Bus (Cservenka & Copping)
VW Golf GTI (Cservenka & Copping)

General
1½-litre GP Racing 1961-1965 (Whitelock)
AC Two-litre Saloons & Buckland Sportscars (Archibald)
Alfa Romeo 155/156/147 Competition Touring Cars (Collins)
Alfa Romeo Giulia Coupé GT & GTA (Tipler)
Alfa Romeo Montreal – The dream car that came true (Taylor)
Alfa Romeo Montreal – The Essential Companion (Classic Reprint of 500 copies) (Taylor)
Alfa Tipo 33 (McDonough & Collins)
Alpine & Renault – The Development of the Revolutionary Turbo F1 Car 1968 to 1979 (Smith)
Alpine & Renault – The Sports Prototypes 1963 to 1969 (Smith)
Alpine & Renault – The Sports Prototypes 1973 to 1978 (Smith)
Anatomy of the Classic Mini (Huthert & Ely)
Anatomy of the Works Minis (Moylan)
Armstrong-Siddeley (Smith)
Art Deco and British Car Design (Down)
Autodrome (Collins & Ireland)
Automotive A-Z, Lane's Dictionary of Automotive Terms (Lane)
Automotive Mascots (Kay & Springate)
Bahamas Speed Weeks, The (O'Neil)
Bentley Continental, Corniche and Azure (Bennett)
Bentley MkVI, Rolls-Royce Silver Wraith, Dawn & Cloud/Bentley R & S-Series (Nutland)
Bluebird CN7 (Stevens)
BMC Competitions Department Secrets (Turner, Chambers & Browning)
BMW 5-Series (Cranswick)
BMW Z-Cars (Taylor)
British at Indianapolis, The (Wagstaff)
British Cars, The Complete Catalogue of, 1895-1975 (Culshaw & Horrobin)
BRM – A Mechanic's Tale (Salmon)
BRM V16 (Ludvigsen)
Bugatti – The 8-cylinder Touring Cars 1920-34 (Price & Arbey)
Bugatti Type 40 (Price)
Bugatti 46/50 Updated Edition (Price & Arbey)
Bugatti T44 & T49 (Price & Arbey)
Bugatti 57 2nd Edition (Price)
Bugatti Type 57 Grand Prix – A Celebration (Tomlinson)
Caravan, Improve & Modify Your (Porter)
Caravans, The Illustrated History 1919-1959 (Jenkinson)
Caravans, The Illustrated History From 1960 (Jenkinson)
Carrera Panamericana, La (Tipler)
Car-tastrophes – 80 automotive atrocities from the past 20 years (Honest John, Fowler)
Chrysler 300 – America's Most Powerful Car 2nd Edition (Ackerson)
Chrysler PT Cruiser (Ackerson)
Citroën DS (Bobbitt)
Classic British Car Electrical Systems (Astley)
Cobra – The Real Thing! (Legate)
Competition Car Aerodynamics 3rd Edition (McBeath)
Competition Car Composites A Practical Handbook (Revised 2nd Edition) (McBeath)
Concept Cars, How to illustrate and design – New 2nd Edition (Dewey)
Cortina – Ford's Bestseller (Robson)
Cosworth – The Search for Power (6th edition) (Robson)
Coventry Climax Racing Engines (Hammill)
Daily Mirror 1970 World Cup Rally 40, The (Robson)
Daimler SP250 New Edition (Long)
Datsun Fairlady Roadster to 280ZX – The Z-Car Story (Long)
Dino – The V6 Ferrari (Long)
Dodge Challenger & Plymouth Barracuda (Grist)
Dodge Charger – Enduring Thunder (Ackerson)
Dodge Dynamite! (Grist)
Dorset from the Sea – The Jurassic Coast from Lyme Regis to Old Harry Rocks photographed from its best viewpoint (also Souvenir Edition) (Belasco)
Draw & Paint Cars – How to (Gardiner)
Drive on the Wild Side, A – 20 Extreme Driving Adventures From Around the World (Weaver)
Dune Buggy, Building A – The Essential Manual (Shakespeare)
Dune Buggy Files (Hale)
Dune Buggy Handbook (Hale)
East German Motor Vehicles in Pictures (Suhr/Weinreich)
Fast Ladies – Female Racing Drivers 1888 to 1970 (Bouzanquet)
Fate of the Sleeping Beauties, The (op de Weegh/Hottendorff/op de Weegh)
Ferrari 288 GTO, The Book of the (Sackey)
Ferrari 333 SP (O'Neil)
Fiat & Abarth 124 Spider & Coupé (Tipler)
Fiat & Abarth 500 & 600 – 2nd Edition (Bobbitt)
Fiats, Great Small (Ward)
Ford Cleveland 335-Series V8 engine 1970 to 1982 – The Essential Source Book (Hammill)
Ford F100/F150 Pick-up 1948-1996 (Ackerson)
Ford F150 Pick-up 1997-2005 (Ackerson)
Ford Focus WRC (Robson)
Ford GT – Then, and Now (Streather)
Ford GT40 (Legate)
Ford Midsize Muscle – Fairlane, Torino & Ranchero (Cranswick)
Ford Model Y (Roberts)
Ford Small Block V8 Racing Engines 1962-1970 – The Essential Source Book (Hammill)
Ford Thunderbird From 1954, The Book of the (Long)
Formula One - The Real Score? (Harvey)
Formula 5000 Motor Racing, Back then ... and back now (Lawson)
Forza Minardi! (Vigar)
France: the essential guide for car enthusiasts – 200 things for the car enthusiast to see and do (Parish)
Grand Prix Ferrari – The Years of Enzo Ferrari's Power, 1948-1980 (Pritchard)
Grand Prix Ford – DFV-powered Formula 1 Cars (Robson)
GT – The World's Best GT Cars 1953-73 (Dawson)
Hillclimbing & Sprinting – The Essential Manual (Short & Wilkinson)
Honda NSX (Long)
Inside the Rolls-Royce & Bentley Styling Department – 1971 to 2001 (Hull)
Intermeccanica – The Story of the Prancing Bull (McCredie & Reisner)
Jaguar, The Rise of (Price)
Jaguar XJ 220 – The Inside Story (Moreton)
Jeep CJ (Ackerson)
Jeep Wrangler (Ackerson)
The Jowett Jupiter – The car that leaped to fame (Nankivell)
Karmann-Ghia Coupé & Convertible (Bobbitt)
Kris Meeke – Intercontinental Rally Challenge Champion (McBride)
Lamborghini Miura Bible, The (Sackey)
Lamborghini Urraco, The Book of the (Landsem)
Lancia 037 (Collins)
Lancia Delta HF Integrale (Blaettel & Wagner)
Land Rover Series III Reborn (Porter)
Land Rover, The Half-ton Military (Cook)
Le Mans Panoramic (Ireland)
Lexus Story, The (Long)
Little book of microcars, the (Quellin)
Little book of smart, the – New Edition (Jackson)
Little book of trikes, the (Quellin)
Lola – The Illustrated History (1957-1977) (Starkey)
Lola – All the Sports Racing & Single-seater Racing Cars 1978-1997 (Starkey)
Lola T70 – The Racing History & Individual Chassis Record – 4th Edition (Starkey)
Lotus 18 Colin Chapman's U-turn (Whitelock)
Lotus 49 (Oliver)
Marketingmobiles, The Wonderful Wacky World of (Hale)
Maserati 250F In Focus (Pritchard)
Mazda MX-5/Miata 1.6 Enthusiast's Workshop Manual (Grainger & Shoemark)
Mazda MX-5/Miata 1.8 Enthusiast's Workshop Manual (Grainger & Shoemark)
Mazda MX-5 Miata, The book of the – The 'Mk1' NA-series 1988 to 1997 (Long)
Mazda MX-5 Miata Roadster (Long)
Mazda Rotary-engined Cars (Cranswick)
Maximum Mini (Booij)
Meet the English (Bowie)
Mercedes-Benz SL – R230 series 2001 to 2011 (Long)
Mercedes-Benz SL – W113-series 1963-1971 (Long)
Mercedes-Benz SL & SLC – 107-series 1971-1989 (Long)
Mercedes-Benz SLK – R170 series 1996-2004 (Long)
Mercedes-Benz SLK – R171 series 2004-2011 (Long)
Mercedes-Benz W123-series – All models 1976 to 1986 (Long)
Mercedes G-Wagen (Long)
MGA (Price Williams)
MGB & MGB GT– Expert Guide (Auto-doc Series) (Williams)
MGB Electrical Systems Updated & Revised Edition (Astley)
Micro Caravans (Jenkinson)
Micro Trucks (Mort)
Microcars at Large! (Quellin)
Mini Cooper – The Real Thing! (Tipler)
Mini Minor to Asia Minor (West)
Mitsubishi Lancer Evo, The Road Car & WRC Story (Long)
Montlhéry, The Story of the Paris Autodrome (Boddy)
Morgan Maverick (Lawrence)
Morgan 3 Wheeler – back to the future!, The (Dron)
Morris Minor, 60 Years on the Road (Newell)
Motor Movies – The Posters! (Veysey)
Motor Racing – Reflections of a Lost Era (Carter)
Motor Racing – The Pursuit of Victory 1930-1962 (Carter)
Motor Racing – The Pursuit of Victory 1963-1972 (Wyatt/Sears)
Motor Racing Heroes – The Stories of 100 Greats (Newman)
Motorhomes, The Illustrated History (Jenkinson)
Motorsport In colour, 1950s (Wainwright)
N.A.R.T. – A concise history of the North American Racing Team 1957 to 1983 (O'Neil)
Nissan 300ZX & 350Z – The Z-Car Story (Long)
Nissan GT-R Supercar: Born to race (Gorodji)
Northeast American Sports Car Races 1950-1959 (O'Neil)
Nothing Runs – Misadventures in the Classic, Collectable & Exotic Car Biz (Slutsky)
Pass the Theory and Practical Driving Tests (Gibson & Hoole)
Pontiac Firebird – New 3rd Edition (Cranswick)
Porsche Boxster (Long)
Porsche 356 (2nd Edition) (Long)
Porsche 908 (Födisch, Neßhöver, Roßbach, Schwarz & Roßbach)
Porsche 911 Carrera – The Last of the Evolution (Corlett)
Porsche 911R, RS & RSR, 4th Edition (Starkey)
Porsche 911, The Book of the (Long)
Porsche 911 – The Definitive History 2004-2012 (Long)
Porsche – The Racing 914s (Smith)
Porsche 911SC 'Super Carrera' – The Essential Companion (Streather)
Porsche 914 & 914-6: The Definitive History of the Road & Competition Cars (Long)
Porsche 924 (Long)
The Porsche 924 Carreras – evolution to excellence (Smith)
Porsche 928 (Long)
Porsche 944 (Long)
Porsche 964, 993 & 996 Data Plate Code Breaker (Streather)
Porsche 993 'King Of Porsche' – The Essential Companion (Streather)
Porsche 996 'Supreme Porsche' – The Essential Companion (Streather)
Porsche 997 2004-2012 – Porsche Excellence (Streather)
Porsche Racing Cars – 1953 to 1975 (Long)
Porsche Racing Cars – 1976 to 2005 (Long)
Porsche – The Rally Story (Meredith)
Porsche: Three Generations of Genius (Meredith)
Preston Tucker & Others (Linde)
RAC Rally Action! (Gardiner)
Racing Colours – Motor Racing Compositions 1908-2009 (Newman)
Rallye Sport Fords: The Inside Story (Moreton)
Renewable Energy Home Handbook, The (Porter)
Roads with a View – England's greatest views and how to find them by road (Corfield)
Rolls-Royce Silver Shadow/Bentley T Series Corniche & Camargue – Revised & Enlarged Edition (Bobbitt)
Rolls-Royce Silver Spirit, Silver Spur & Bentley Mulsanne 2nd Edition (Bobbitt)
Rootes Cars of the 50s, 60s & 70s – Hillman, Humber, Singer, Sunbeam & Talbot (Rowe)
Rover P4 (Bobbitt)
Runways & Racers (O'Neil)
Russian Motor Vehicles – Soviet Limousines 1930-2003 (Kelly)
Russian Motor Vehicles – The Czarist Period 1784 to 1917 (Kelly)
RX-7 – Mazda's Rotary Engine Sportscar (Updated & Revised New Edition) (Long)
Singer Story: Cars, Commercial Vehicles, Bicycles & Motorcycle (Atkinson)
Sleeping Beauties USA – abandoned classic cars & trucks (Marek)
SM – Citroën's Maserati-engined Supercar (Long & Claverol)
Speedway – Auto racing's ghost tracks (Collins & Ireland)
Sprite Caravans, The Story of (Jenkinson)
Standard Motor Company, The Book of the (Robson)
Steve Hole's Kit Car Cornucopia – Cars, Companies, Stories, Facts & Figures: the UK's kit car scene since 1949 (Hole)
Subaru Impreza: The Road Car And WRC Story (Long)
Supercar, How to Build your own (Thompson)
Tales from the Toolbox (Oliver)
Tatra – The Legacy of Hans Ledwinka, Updated & Enlarged Collector's Edition of 1500 copies (Margolius & Henry)
Taxi! The Story of the 'London' Taxicab (Bobbitt)
To Boldly Go – twenty six vehicle designs that dared to be different (Hull)
Toleman Story, The (Hilton)
Toyota Celica & Supra, The Book of Toyota's Sports Coupés (Long)
Toyota MR2 Coupés & Spyders (Long)
Triumph TR6 (Kimberley)
Two Summers – The Mercedes-Benz W196R Racing Car (Ackerson)
TWR Story, The – Group A (Hughes & Scott)
Unraced (Collins)
Volkswagen Bus Book, The (Bobbitt)
Volkswagen Bus or Van to Camper, How to Convert (Porter)
Volkswagens of the World (Glen)
VW Beetle Cabriolet – The full story of the convertible Beetle (Bobbitt)
VW Beetle – The Car of the 20th Century (Copping)
VW Bus – 40 Years of Splitties, Bays & Wedges (Copping)
VW Bus Book, The (Bobbitt)
VW Golf: Five Generations of Fun (Copping & Cservenka)
VW – The Air-cooled Era (Copping)
VW T5 Camper Conversion Manual (Porter)
VW Campers (Copping)
Volkswagen Type 3, The book of the – Concept, Design, International Production Models & Development (Glen)
Volvo Estate, The (Hollebone)
You & Your Jaguar XK8/XKR – Buying, Enjoying, Maintaining, Modifying – New Edition (Thorley)
Which Oil? – Choosing the right oils & greases for your antique, vintage, veteran, classic or collector car (Michell)
Wolseley Cars 1948 to 1975 (Rowe)
Works Minis, The Last (Purves & Brenchley)
Works Rally Mechanic (Moylan)

Veloce's other imprints:
Hubble & Hattie   Belvedere

Also available ... Apps Download now from www.digital.veloce.co.uk
Also available ... eBook Download now from www.digital.veloce.co.uk

www.veloce.co.uk

First published in April 2006 by Veloce Publishing Limited, Veloce House, Parkway Farm Business Park, Middle Farm Way, Poundbury, Dorchester DT1 3AR, England. Fax 01305 250479 / e-mail info@veloce.co.uk / web www.veloce.co.uk or www.velocebooks.com.
Reprinted June 2017. ISBN: 978-1-787111-23-3; UPC: 6-36847-01123-9.

British Library Cataloguing in Publication Data – A catalogue record for this book is available from the British Library.
Typesetting, design and page make-up all by Veloce Publishing Ltd on Apple Mac. Printed and bound by CPI Group (UK) Ltd, Croydon, CR0 4YY.

VW BUS

Forty years of Splitties, Bays & Wedges

By Richard Copping

VELOCE PUBLISHING
THE PUBLISHER OF FINE AUTOMOTIVE BOOKS

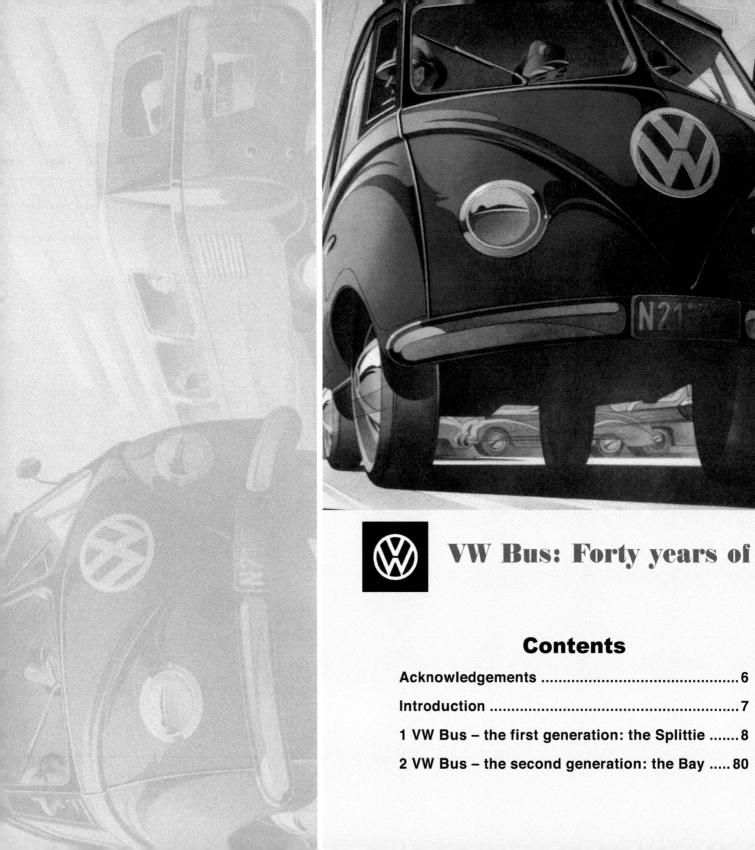

VW Bus: Forty years of

Contents

Splitties, Bays and Wedges

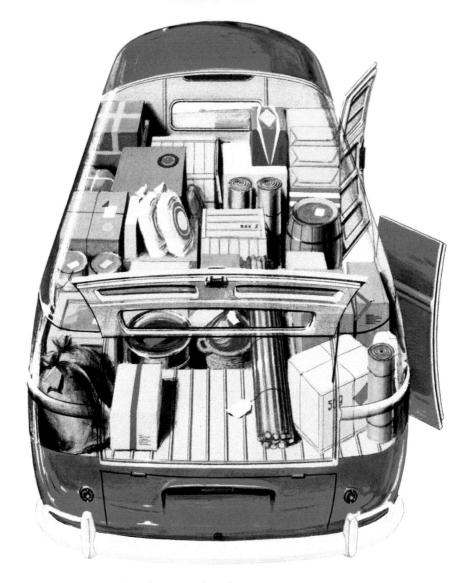

Acknowledgements

That this book is as comprehensive as it is in terms of illustrative material is due in no small measure to five fellow Volkswagen enthusiasts. Many years ago Raymond Lynn, once an independent Volkswagen dealer, donated his entire collection of brochures to me; this kind gesture triggered my interest in the wonderful artwork contained within Volkswagen's promotional material of the 1950s, and the equally inspirational and clever photography of the following decade. Over the last few show seasons, Matt Harrison has managed to track down an incredible number of unusual and rare brochures for me. Neal Dorfman, from the USA, proved an invaluable source when it came to locating suitably attractive material for inclusion in this book, particularly relating to later Bay models and the Vanagon. An old friend with the Volkswagen collecting habit, Vic Kaye, let me have a good number of items at the same prices he had paid for them. Last, but by no means least, Brian Screaton not only supplied several rare and fascinating brochures to add to my collection, but also loaned two or three items that I hadn't been able to track down for love nor money. Without this material the story of the first 40 years of the VW Bus would have lacked a vital ingredient. Many, many thanks to them all. Finally, thanks also go to my old pal and fellow *VW Motoring* editor, Ken Cservenka, who scoured the text for gremlins, a task he's particularly adept at!

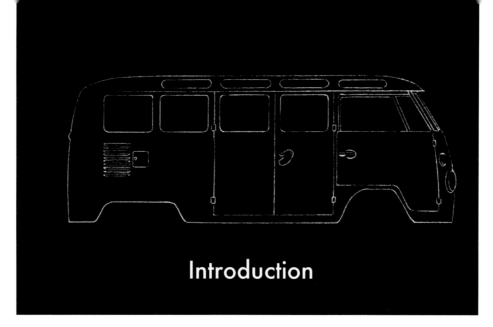

Introduction

'I started with a simple plan.'

"It all began with the notion that a wagon should hold a lot, and no notion of how it should look. So when we sat down to design the VW Station Wagon we started by drawing a big box with 170 cubic feet of space. This gave us room to seat nine people comfortably and 13 pieces of luggage. Once we got the people in we couldn't just let them sit there in a dark box. So we cut 21 windows to let the light in, a big hole to put the luggage in, and four doors to let the people out. To make the things go, we put the air-cooled Volkswagen engine in the back. And what we ended up with is ... a wagon that holds a lot, parks easily and doesn't drink much gas. What could be simpler than that?"

US ad agency DDB – wit and wisdom personified.

In the slightly adapted words of US advertising agency Doyle Dane Bernbach (DDB), "I started with a simple plan" when plotting the course of this book – a volume encompassing the first three generations of Volkswagen's hugely popular Bus. Other books have covered the ubiquitous Bus in varying degrees of detail, but nobody has built the story of 40 years of Transporter production entirely around contemporary archive material.

This simple but original concept immediately allows us all to marvel at the enormous talent of Volkswagen's pet artist of the 1950s – Bernd Reuters and his skilful beautification of what, after all, was rightly described as little more than a box on wheels. With a change of decade, along came the US advertising agency DDB and a revolution in text style – from the frankly dull unemotional sentences of the average copywriter to a staccato approach and incredible straight talking. Out went Herr Reuters and in came what appeared to be attractively simple photography. DDB and its followers were successfully selling the Bus on a ticket of honesty.

Come the high-noon of 1967, out went the first generation of Bus to be replaced by a new all-singing, all-dancing replacement. Within nine-months of its launch the architect of Volkswagen's phenomenal post-war success, Heinz Nordhoff, was dead and, while it took a few years to show would-be purchasers of Volkswagen products a completely new face, perhaps by coincidence the powers of influence held by DDB seemed to melt away and a less convincing breed of Bus image began to emerge.

Compiling compelling images of the second generation of Volkswagen Bus is nowhere near as easy as it is for the first. Thank goodness there is an easy availability of material from America – a land where imagery, at least for Volkswagen products, remained high on the agenda. As for the third generation of Transporter, a selection of worthwhile photographs and layouts proved even more challenging and, while theoretically each generation of Bus demands something approaching equal representation in the book, an image or two had to be stretched in Chapter Three!

Having chosen the artwork – photographic or otherwise – all that was necessary was to tell the Bus's fascinating tale in an innovative manner. Simplicity itself: replicate the layout and font style of the original brochures throughout, adding text covering marketing, sales and history – to name but three subjects – and wrap it up in a style some academics would never wish to be associated with!

However, one final issue remained – Volkswagen's 'box on wheels' hadn't really got a name, merely a model type. Transporter might sound official, while Bus could well be endearing to all, but, with the best will in the world, such titles didn't help in the great generation identification game. The answer had to be to adopt enthusiasts' terminology and thus the first model, the Splittie, or split windscreen, was succeeded by the panoramic screen Bay, which in turn gave way to the Wedge – a self explanatory description of the vehicle's shape if ever there was one. This last little local difficulty resolved – a simple plan it was and is!

 ## 1. Birth of the Splittie

Let's set the record straight immediately – the Splittie is a postwar creation without the Beetle's links to Volkswagen's dubious Nazi past. With the KdF-Wagen's designer, Ferdinand Porsche, in enforced exile and all his ties to the rebirth of the Wolfsburg factory severed, other catalysts fused to create the Splittie. Without denigrating the great man's name, his best attempt at producing a commercial vehicle had resulted in a creation that appeared similar to a chopped Beetle with a garden shed slung unceremoniously across its hind section. A disparate alliance comprised of a Yorkshireman with an unequalled talent for improvisation, an entrepreneurial Dutchman and a German industrialist who would turn a shaky and faltering business into one of the key players in the automotive industry throughout the world, led to the creation of the Splittie.

With the withdrawal of British Army transport used for trundling parts from one area of the Beetle assembly line to another, Major Ivan Hirst, the officer in charge of the occupied and re-named Wolfsburg Motor Works, devised a flat-bed truck, utilising the chassis of a Kübelwagen (the military go anywhere incarnation of the KdF-Wagen) and Beetle running gear, topped off with a simple box-like cab. Known as the Plattenwagen, this vehicle with the operator's seat over the rear-mounted engine, was easy to manoeuvre, afforded plentiful carrying space and inevitably caught the eye of the extrovert Ben Pon – the official Dutch importer of the Beetle.

Inspired by the notion of a vehicle that had been purpose-built to perform a specific task (unlike all contemporaries and Porsche's long since defunct adapted KdF-Wagen with garden shed), Pon first tried to import the Plattenwagen to his home country. Foiled by the Dutch Transport authorities, who decreed that a driver must sit at the front of a vehicle, an undeterred Pon sketched out his thoughts for a purpose-built cargo van. Crude in its execution, nevertheless the simple pencil outline bore an uncanny resemblance to the Splittie. Hirst liked what Pon presented, but both men were to be frustrated, as Colonel Radclyffe, charged with overall responsibility for engineering construction in the British zone, decreed that resources were already over-stretched, turning the 'box-on-wheels' down in the process.

The arrival of Heinz Nordhoff as Director General of Volkswagen in January 1948, some seven months later, ensured that the concept had merely been shelved and not lost forever.

From concept to reality

That Nordhoff had an incredible challenge ahead of him to make Volkswagen and its sole product economically viable seems to have had little bearing on his determination to push ahead with Pon's idea for a second product when it was re-presented in the autumn of 1948. Perhaps, as a former director of Opel's truck division, he recognised the drawing's potential merit and unique nature in a sluggish marketplace devoid of inspirational or practical applications.

Giving Alfred Haesner, the factory's Technical Director, the go-ahead to start plan EA-7, development project No7 – the Transporter – Nordhoff's brief was that all preconceived ideas of what a delivery van should contain must be ignored.

By November 20th 1948, two designs had been presented to an impatient Nordhoff: one with a straight, flat driver's cab, which he dismissed, and a second, with a slightly raked front, that was given the go-ahead. With cost considerations paramount, as many Beetle parts as possible were utilised, including the car's 25hp engine and crash gearbox. That the new body was bolted straight onto a widened Beetle chassis, complete with both torsion bars and running gear, was its downfall. Within three weeks of completion of the first prototype on March 9th 1949, testing had to be halted.

The Beetle's chassis proved totally unsuited to its new task, being unable to withstand the increased stresses, twisting and folding when weight was placed in the load carrying section. The design department set about rebuilding the first prototype and added a second, featuring what was essentially a unitary design, with two hefty longitudinal members and robust supporting outriggers. Following Nordhoff's decree that production

The Volkswagen Transporter offers much more
panel surface for advertising.
Close-up view of the road increases driving safety in city traffic.

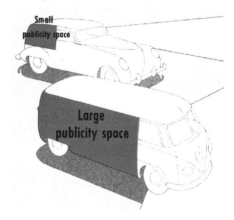

of the Transporter would begin at the latest on December 1st 1949, so that the new model could be delivered at the beginning of 1950, testing re-commenced towards the end of May.

A reduction drive, similar to that of the Kübelwagen, gave a suitable transmission ratio and better ground clearance, while cost-saving dual torsion bars were used for the back axle. Nordhoff personally suggested many options and improvements, and while one prototype was subjected to 12,000km of testing over the worst roads that could be found and passed with flying colours, others had to follow which not only incorporated his refinements, but also took account of the plan to launch not just a delivery vehicle, but also a pick-up, an eight-seater microbus and even options suitable for use by the ambulance service and post office.

On November 12th, Nordhoff's project was presented to the press. It lacked one ingredient, one which perhaps didn't seem important at the time – the vehicle lacked a name, being simply referred to as the Type 2 Transporter. Nordhoff nevertheless sold this "unitised body, with the main characteristics of a Volkswagen" in a most convincing manner. It would be built without compromises. "This is why we did not start from an available chassis, but from the cargo space," he said. "With this van and only this van, the cargo space lies exactly between the axles. The driver sits in the front and there is equal weight in the back, due to the fuel tank and engine; that is the best compromise. The famous cab above engine [design] gave such horrendous handling characteristics that we never even considered it. You can tell by the state of the trees in the British zone how well the British army lorries, built on this principle, handle on wet roads when they are not loaded."

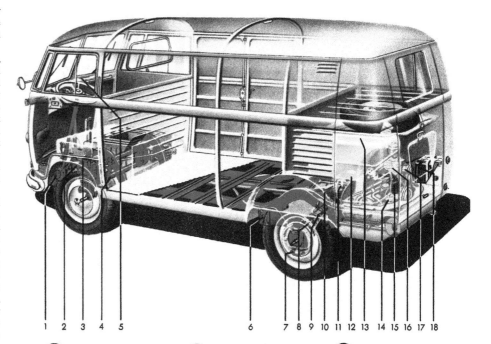

| 1 2 3 4 5 | 6 | 7 8 9 10 11 12 13 14 15 16 17 18 |

1 Steering gear   7 Brake wheel cylinder   13 Fuel tank

2 Brake master cylinder   8 Spur reduction gearing   14 Fuel pump

3 Front shock absorber   9 Rear axle   15 Distributor

4 Front axle   10 Transmission   16 Carburetor

5 Defroster vent   11 Fuel tap   17 Generator

6 Torsion bar mounting   12 Starter   18 Battery

Thanks to perfect distribution of weight with the engine in the rear counterbalancing the driver in the front, even when empty the Volkswagen glides as smoothly over rough roads as a swan on a pond.

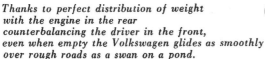

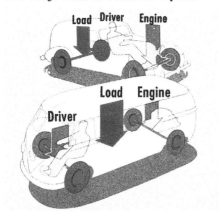

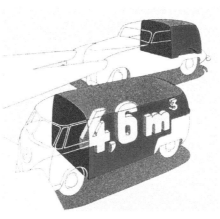

Just glance at the measurements of the loading spaces and you will find that they speak for themselves.

HANNOVER

MIT 40 l BRENNSTOFF
430 km AKTIONSRADIUS

KASSEL

FULDA

WÜRZBURG

NÜRNBERG

Designed to "revolutionise the truck industry"

Sales

Launched at the Geneva Motor Show in March 1950, after a selection of Volkswagen's most important customers had been afforded access to a series of test-drive vehicles produced during February, initial manufacture amounted to just 10 vehicles daily. During the remaining 9 months of 1950, 8059 Type 2 Transporters of three types and two paint finishes were unleashed on a mesmerised public. The straightforward Panelvan accounted for 70 per cent of production, while the equally revolutionary Kombi and more luxurious Microbus each amounted to around 15 per cent. While the majority were painted in rich glossy finishes, 2941 received nothing more than coats of primer … all will be revealed!

Marketing

Although a brochure to promote the versatility of the Splittie had been available virtually from its launch, a much more artistic approach was introduced in December 1950 with Volkswagen employing the talented artist Bernd Reuters to stylise and streamline its products. Sadly, the Volkswagen 'Archive' knows little of the artist's background or influence. Enthusiasts will pay a comparative fortune to acquire examples of his highly collectable handiwork today. While many assume that such a style was unique to the brand, in reality Volkswagen was merely following a trend, with long forgotten manufacturers like DKW, Wiking, Gutbrad and Goliath also producing material that relied on the skills of artists to promote their products.

10-51 TB 202a-20 · Änderungen vorbehalten · Printed in Germany · Druckerei H. Osterwald, Hannover

km/h

100000

80 0

60 20

40

AUTOBAHN-
DAUERGESCHWINDIGKEIT

WENDEKREISRADIUS

5,5 m

STEIGFÄ

Specification

Air-cooled, horizontally-opposed four cylinders

Capacity	1131cc
Bore and stroke	75mm x 64mm
Compression ratio	5.8:1
Maximum power	25bhp at 3300rpm
Maximum torque	67Nm at 2000rpm
Carb	Type 26VFI or VFJ downdraught Solex
Gears	Four-speed without synchromesh
Front suspension	Transverse torsion bars, parallel trailing arms, telescopic dampers
Rear suspension	Transverse torsion bars, trailing arms, telescopic dampers & swinging half axles
Wheels and tyres	16in diameter, 5.60 x 16 tyres
Overall length	159in
Overall width	66in
Overall height	73.5in
Unladen weight	18cwt
Maximum speed	50mph
0-40mph	22.7secs
Fuel consumption	Around 25mpg

Visit Veloce on the web
www.veloce.co.uk

EIT
1.GANG 23%
2.GANG 13%
3.GANG 7%
4.GANG 3,5%

BEI VOLLER BELASTUNG

13

2. FAMILY PLANNING

 ## VW Lieferwagen – Delivery or Panelvan

Bei einem Minimum an Anschaffungs- und Unterhaltungskosten bietet der VW-Lieferwagen seinem Besitzer all das, was er von einem Transportfahrzeug der schnellen Klasse erwartet: Überraschend große Geräumigkeit und Tragkraft mit vielen Variationsmöglichkeiten für die Aufteilung des Laderaumes je nach Verwendungszweck, eine gefällige Form mit großen, ungebrochenen Außenflächen für wirkungsvolle Werbebeschriftung und alle Voraussetzungen für einen flinken und wendigen Einsatz im Großstadtgewühl wie auch für zuverlässige Robustheit im Überlandverkehr — selbst auf schlechten Wegen. Die weit zu öffnenden Flügeltüren geben einen sehr bequemen Zugang zum Laderaum frei, der durch einen Ganzstahlaufbau hervorragend geschützt und durch seine Lage zwischen den Achsen bestens gefedert ist.

A great deal of the story of the birth of the Splittie is the same as that of the Panelvan. Characteristics at launch included an enormous rear hatch, which gave access to a cavernous compartment containing the vehicle's diminutive engine and battery. Additionally it was home to the spare wheel and the fuel tank which, apart from being filled from within the area, was also precariously balanced above and to the left of the power unit.

The massive hatch, which later inevitably gave rise to the 'barn door' nickname for all early models didn't give access to the interior loading space, while a colossal VW roundel (which was discontinued in the dying months of 1950) demonstrated that Volkswagen wished to shout loud and clear that this was its product. Panelvans lacked a rear bumper at launch and would continue so to do until the end of 1953.

Thanks to the lack of rearward access, the brochure copywriters had to sell the advantages of side loading, a task at which they were reasonably adept: "It is easy to load even the bulkiest goods through the spacious double side doors. The large floor of the vehicle is just a few inches above the pavement and it is flat like a table. You can stand in the doorway and reach every corner of the vehicle, thus avoiding all that running back and forth so necessary in rear-loading vans." Nevertheless, conscious of the lack of a rear loading facility, by late June 1951, an optional second set of cargo doors was offered, allowing easy loading from either side of the Panelvan.

Designed to lug objects weighing up to three-quarters of a ton or bulky enough to occupy 162ft³ of loading space, the copywriters were proud to stress "the ratio of payload to truck weight is excellent," while adding that "the Volkswagen hauls a payload almost as great as its own weight." Later brochure drawings (such as that reproduced on page six) would show the Panelvan loaded to the gunnels, apparently without adverse effect.

Although a 25bhp motor with a top speed of 50mph was not at variance with the Transporter's contemporaries, Volkswagen was eager to address any sense of sluggishness when the vehicle was fully laden. At prototype stage, reduction boxes, utilising a separate oil supply and housing a pair of reduction gears, were adopted and located on the outer ends of the axle tubes. Such devices had first been used on Porsche's Kübelwagen to allow the military version of the Beetle to accelerate more easily when the going underfoot was difficult, or to pull better when fully loaded. Complex undoubtedly, but both effective and inexpensive compared to other options.

To make the paint-shop's life as simple as possible, the Panelvan was available in just one colour – the not unattractive shade of Dove Blue (Taubenblau L31), an option that would remain on the cards throughout Splittie production. Amazingly though, some 46 per cent of vans were delivered to their new owners wearing nothing more than a coat of primer, but as hinted at previously, there was a reason.

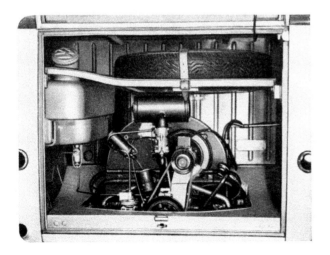

 **Kombi**

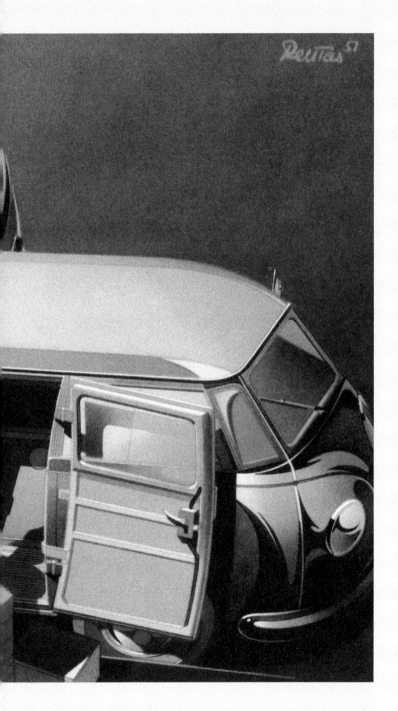

"Take out the seats and it is an efficient delivery van suitable for quick service of any kind ... put the roomy, well-cushioned seats into the Volkswagen Kombi and it is a comfortable passenger vehicle seating eight."

Hot on the heels of the Panelvan came two further Splittie options, the Kombi and the Microbus. The former made its debut on May 16th, the latter on the 22nd. The Kombi was immediately distinguishable externally from its lowlier Panelvan brother thanks to the insertion of three rectangular windows along each of its sides (at the time it lacked a rear window). Initially similar to so many vehicles on the roads today, the Kombi and other models benefited from a rear window with effect from April 1951. Such was its importance that Reuters was soon commissioned to illustrate this talking point, doing so particularly effectively in the drawing used to accompany the contents listing on pages 4 and 5.

More windows implies more seats, and this was indeed what the Kombi had to offer: furniture that could be quickly removed at the turn of a few wing nuts. With three sardined onto the bench seat in the cab, another six adults could expect to be accommodated in the Kombi's Spartan interior, even though Volkswagen's advertising gurus restricted the overall number count to a more comfortable eight. Flexibility was the name of the game, for, with the removal of just the centre row of seats, the Kombi could still seat five, possibly six, while also carrying smaller deliveries. As such, the Kombi was unquestionably the world's first true multi-purpose vehicle – a versatility immediately rewarded with popularity.

From the Kombi's initial stake holding of 15 per cent of total Splittie sales, it crept up to a figure in excess of 20 per cent in year two, a position it would continue to hold not only throughout the remaining years of the decade, but also to the end of first generation production some 17 years later.

With the Kombi's accoutrements laid bare, the additional cost over that of the Panelvan was easily explained, just as its overall lack of deluxe features explained the 'discounted' nature of its selling price when compared to both the Microbus and another even more elaborate option which made its debut in June 1951.

"The Volkswagen Kombi is, in every sense ... two efficient money-earning vehicles in one."

Passengers seated in what doubled as the Kombi's loading area rested their feet on rubber matting. Contrary to Volkswagen's re-assurance that the seats were 'well-cushioned', here were basic benches and backrests. As for the rest, the Kombi followed to the letter the package offered in a Panelvan, lacking any form of headlining or interior panelling, instead offering its occupants a view of acres of painted metal. Upfront, the cab sported a basic headlining plus door-cards, each made of plain fibreboard.

Although plainly austere, a few features helped to take the knife-edge off the Kombi's basic apparel, at least if the copywriters were to be believed. First, there was the cut-down dividing 'wall' between the cab and the loading compartment, reducing the Panelvan's 'us-and-them' set-up to a minimum. Second, the copywriters drew attention to the "eight side windows and the large panoramic front window [making] the interior bright and cheerful". Hmm! Or how about these valiant attempts at whitewash? "The décor is deliberately simple and

completely suited to changing tastes, for the loading area must be quickly and easily cleanable ... The interior furnishings are completely designed for practical utility; goods that leave dirt behind need not be avoided, for the interior is as easy and handy to clean as it is quick to change into a people carrier." However, Volkswagen's blossoming marketing team's ingenuity reached as yet unparalleled heights when it christened the most extraordinary of extra selling points: "the six side windows can be easily made into as many travelling show windows for your merchandise. It is extremely effective advertising that costs you nothing!"

Although more generally associated with the lordliest of Transporter options, the relatively humble Kombi was depicted in

V O L K S W

several brochures sporting a fold-back sunroof, while allegedly from 1953 there was an option to specify a walkway from the cab to the vehicle's interior.

Test-driving a relatively early Kombi, the US publication *Mechanix Illustrated* summarised the vehicle's charm (or lack of it): "You won't need a goat skin from Beaux Arts in Paris to realise this rig has the chic and boulevard appeal of a paratrooper's left boot or a pair of paint splattered overalls. This is a purely functional workhorse and the designers obviously don't give a damn whether it looked like an egg in a washing machine providing it did the work. And that it does."

Thank goodness that for the initially tricky American market, at least, there was something a little more comfortable: the next pea out of the pod, the Microbus!

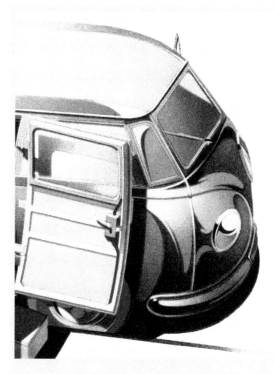

"The vehicle has as many windows as a sight-seeing bus! Notice how comfortable and roomy it is. And of course it has built in heating, too."

G E N W E R K   G M B H

19

VW Kleinbus - the Microbus

①

②

③

④

⑤

⑥

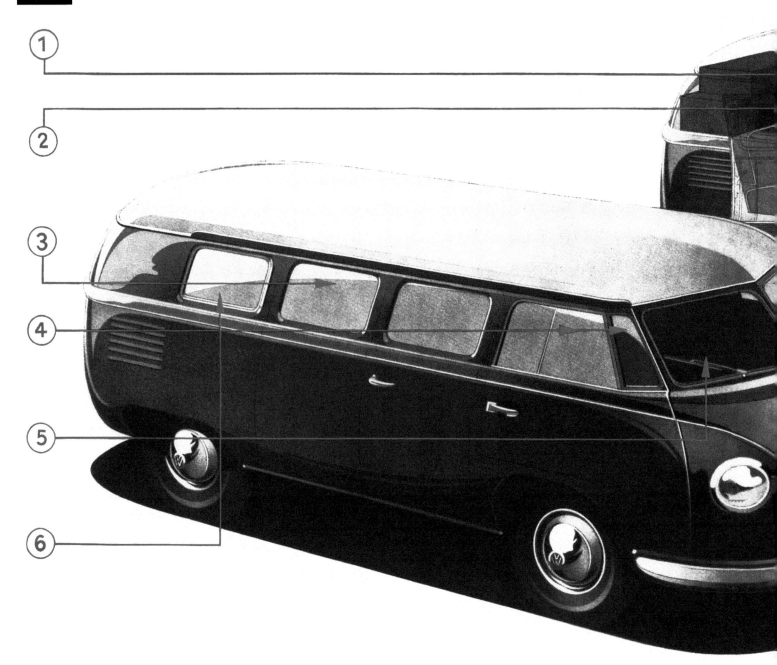

Between its launch towards the end of May 1950 and the arrival of the VW Kleinbus Sonderausführung at the start of June of the following year, the Microbus reigned supreme – almost. There was one problem and it related to confusion regarding branding. Was the vehicle a small bus, the Kleinbus, or was it the VW Achtsitzer?

Unquestionably more deluxe than the Kombi, Nordhoff must have had his eye on the valuable revenue generating benefits of exports when the Microbus's specification was decided upon in Wolfsburg towers. Not only did it feature a full-length cloth headlining, which extended right around the side windows, but

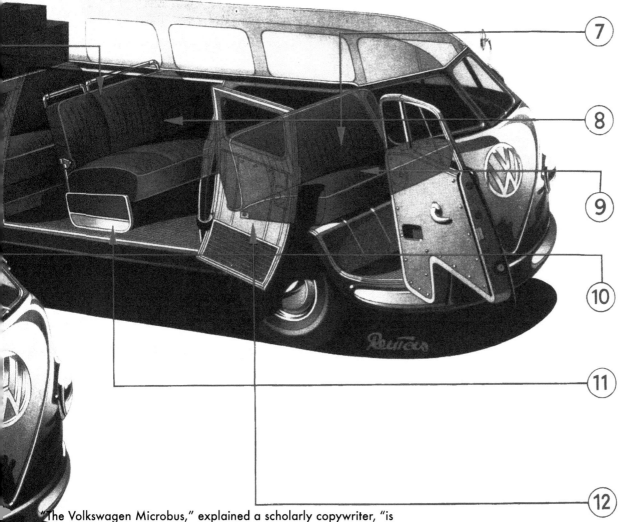

"The Volkswagen Microbus," explained a scholarly copywriter, "is in reality not a bus but an oversize passenger car accommodating eight persons [the VW Achtsitzer]. Every passenger has more head, leg and elbowroom than he needs. There is not another car of its kind so easy to get in and out of as the Volkswagen Microbus and no other in which the passengers are so comfortable, seated well between the axles ... The Volkswagen Microbus is a new type of eight-passenger car for inexpensive travelling. It will pay for itself in savings before you know it."

also a below-the-waistband interior decked out with fibreboard panelling, which extended to the door cards. Opening rear side windows complemented the luxury of the seats, which were finished in both pleated- and piped-vinyl. Although initially the centre bench seat was a static fitment, it wasn't long before it grew a little in length and one third of its backrest could be tipped allowing easier access to the rear seats. "The tilting seat makes it easy to reach the rear seats. Access even to the seat in the far corner is unhindered."

"Whether darting through traffic, skimming along country roads or winding its way through tortuous mountains, the Volkswagen Microbus offers a maximum level of safety."

The Volkswagen Eight-Passenger Micro Bus

is the ideal vehicle for small touring parties.

It is an ideal means of conveyance for quick shuttle service.

It is fine for taxiing people and is extremely economical to operate.

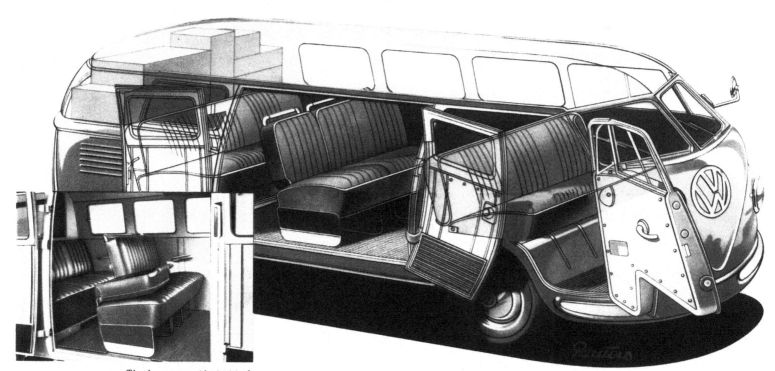

*The doors open wide, invitingly
exposing the comfortable roomy seats.
The tilting seat back facilitates access to the rear seats.*

"The Volkswagen eight-passenger Microbus is the ideal vehicle for small touring parties."

The waistline partition between the cab and the passenger area in the Microbus was fitted with two grab handles, one positioned vertically by the door to assist in clambering aboard the vehicle, the other fixed horizontally to help passengers counter the effects of a driver hurtling his passengers along country roads or darting his way through heavy city traffic. Later, grab handles would adorn the tops of the backrests of the middle row of seats, while, from the start, furnishings such as the chromed finger latch for the cab door sliding window, the double door handle, the substantial coat hooks and even the spherical ashtray were of the highest quality. Perhaps it is also worth stressing here that the Microbus was not intended to double as a delivery van – ever. To hammer home this point, Volkswagen fixed the seats to the floor.

Offered from launch to March 1955 in just two colour scheme options, namely Brown Beige over Light Beige or simply Stone Grey throughout, a percentage of new owners opted to buy the Microbus in primer so that they could adopt a paint scheme compatible with their own personal preferences. Although many Microbuses emerged from the factory fitted with painted hubcaps there was an opportunity to specify chrome using an 'M' code (factory fitted optional equipment or 'mehrausstattung'), an area encountered again shortly.

The Microbus was set to play a prominent role in the Splittie line-up throughout the vehicle's production run and would continue to feature as part of the range in the days of the Bay. Nevertheless, it was always partly eclipsed in luxury terms, if nothing else, by the crème de la crème of Splitties, described overleaf.

"Do you know of any other eight-passenger vehicle that will give you 30 miles per Imperial gallon at a speed of 50 miles per hour or more?"

 VW Microbus Deluxe – Samba

Healthy sales of the Splittie from its launch, and the emergence of a feel-good factor in the German economy linked to success in most markets for the Export (or Deluxe) model of the Beetle, encouraged Nordhoff to plough the profits generated back into Volkswagen. This way he could afford to invest in further projects, one of which was undoubtedly an all-singing, all-dancing version of the Splittie, which made even the previously snooty Microbus appear austere by comparison.

Primarily due to its price, the Sondermodell - now lovingly referred to by enthusiasts as the 'Samba' - never sold in earth-shattering quantities, although it proved a valuable weapon in the great export game from day one. Today it heads the list of the most sought-after models of Transporter from any generation. Nordhoff and his team certainly went to town on the design, and the copywriters rejoiced in the golden opportunity to trumpet the superlatives.

"A harmonious two-colour scheme and a double chromium-plated ornamental band enhance the beauty of the Volkswagen Micro Bus Deluxe. Comfortable deep-cushioned seats and handsome fittings make the vehicle a miniature luxury bus for travel and excursions." And there was more, much more!

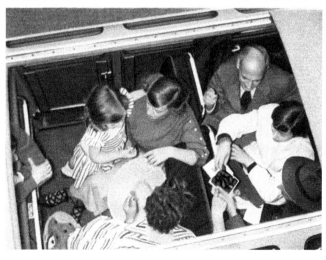

"Many leading airlines use this handsome trim Microbus Deluxe to convey passengers to and from the airports.

"This airline uses the Volkswagen Microbus Deluxe because it wants to give its passengers maximum comfort and economy of transport. No words or pictures can properly convey to you the beauty, comfort and numerous advantages of this remarkable eight-passenger vehicle. You have to see it and drive it yourself to appreciate all its qualities. The Volkswagen Microbus Deluxe equips you to meet any competition. Its stream lines and handsome colours attract the eyes of everyone. Its interior is equally inviting with its eight comfortable seats affording each passenger a panoramic view. Side windows in the roof afford an upward view as well. All the windows are equipped with safety glass ... In good weather you can open the sunroof so that all the passengers can enjoy the fresh air and sunshine. The Volkswagen Microbus Deluxe has the same gliding comfort as the Volkswagen passenger car ..."

"It has an abundance of chromed bright-work, it's airy and light inside thanks to additional windows and a fold-back sunroof, while it has its own unique full cab-width dashboard"

The Samba was previewed in April 1951 at the Frankfurt Motor Show, before going into full production on June 1st. A wealth of features set it aside from the rest of the Splittie pack.

For a start, the interior was brighter and airier than any other option, even the Microbus. Three separate developments brought this about and two of them would remain unique to the Samba throughout its production run. A quick count of the number of side windows behind the cab doors instantly identifies a Samba, because while the Microbus and Kombi sported three, its big brother sports four. Out went the rectangular look and in came the multitudinous square option – instantly eating into the amount of light restricting metalwork in the process. However, it didn't end there.

Exclusive feature number two was the addition of Plexiglas wraparound windows on each rear quarter panel, while four oblong skylights 'glazed' with the same material were cut into each side of the roof panel. Plexiglas was a clear material similar in nature to Perspex, which was also used in the production of aircraft canopies. In Plexiglas proved an ideal solution for an otherwise difficult and expensive deluxe option.

The third item to throw light on the subject was the addition of a fold-back canvas sunroof, manufactured by Golde. It was this item that filtered its way down onto the Microbus and even the Kombi (at extra cost, of course), just as the Standard or basic Beetle could be similarly endowed if the pennies were handed over.

How many vehicles could boast a total of 23 windows with a sunroof thrown in for good measure?

the days when it was a cheaper option to produce two small rear panes for the Beetle, rather than one curved piece of glass and to endow the Splittie with its distinctive frontal split pane screen for the same reasons,

Externally, the Samba was lavished with a magpie's nest of brightwork. Apart from being the only model in the Splittie range to feature chromed hubcaps as standard, until December 1953 it was the one option to benefit from a rear bumper, bestowed with executive rubbing strips encased in shiny mouldings. Additional trim didn't stop there, as chunky polished mouldings bedecked the 'V'-shaped swage lines on the Samba's front, which continued along the cab doors and just below the multitude of side windows. Further mouldings were attached to each side of the vehicle, on the outside of the sills, directly between the two sets of wheels. The Samba was the

only model to feature a plated VW roundel, and exclusivity extended to the paintwork with the exquisite combination of shades described as Chestnut Brown over Sealing Wax Red.

The inside of the Samba was similarly luxurious. Although other models relied on little more than an instrument binnacle, the Samba boasted a full-length dashboard from its launch. (In a general re-vamp in March 1955, all models were fitted with a full length dashboard, albeit of a different design to the original Samba item.) Curiously, the copywriters didn't take full advantage of this obviously deluxe feature, content to state that the vehicle came supplied with "a large instrument panel", was "provided with a [mechanical] clock", while the "dashboard [was] designed to receive a radio, if desired".

Piped and fluted upholstery was used throughout, while a full headlining was inevitable, as was carpeting for the floor of the rear luggage compartment. Protective chromed rails to secure luggage and rubber strips to preserve the carpet, served to indicate a truly first-class finish to this area of the Samba. The backrest of the seat nearest the side-doors was both split from the rest and foldable, allowing much easier access for rear seat passengers. A thoughtful array of coat hooks, grab handles and ashtrays, complemented items like the steering wheel, controls and knobs, which were finished in ivory rather than the more basic-looking black.

The Samba – a premium product, without doubt, but at a premium price too! In 1955, one US dealer jotted down his best prices for a customer on the brochure he was handing out – the Panelvan rolled in at $1930, the Kombi carried a $2130 tag, the Microbus upped the odds at $2230, but the Samba topped the bill at $2685.

 Pick-up

"The Volkswagen Pick-up Truck has what others do not – a lower compartment."

Check out any chronology of Splittie introductions and additions and there it is in black and white: after the Samba, the next variation was the VW Ambulance. However, as will be revealed in a few pages' time, there's a special reason for 'launching' the Pick-up, or Pritschenwagen, at this point in the story. It was virtually 16 months after the debut of the Samba that the workhorse Pick-up made its first appearance, the precise date being August 25th 1952. If the Samba's birth had been prompted by an upturn in the German economy and the need to export a suitably deluxe product, then the reasoning behind the Pick-up's launch was very different. Although the model would prove popular both at home and abroad, here was a variation on the theme designed to fill a gap in the already expanding Splittie range on offer. While the copywriters hadn't quite latched onto startling strap-lines yet, as the heading on this page amply serves to demonstrate, the model was both exciting and desirable to a whole spectrum of trades. Nordhoff knew it would be, and that was why he had been prepared to spend the considerable sums required to amend and adapt the Splittie for picking-up purposes. Thanks to the success of the other models in the range, he had the funds available to finance the substantial changes and re-tooling required.

With a flat-bed as its key asset, it was necessary to both relocate and re-design the fuel tank for the Pick-up. Its new position was above and to the right of the gearbox, which, in turn, resulted in the fuel neck filler being fitted on the right-hand side of the body, in reality a much better location than the fiddly arrangement which remained in use for the rest of the range, involving opening the engine lid to gain access to the refuelling point. The spare wheel also had to be re-housed, moving from a horizontal position above the engine, to a special well conveniently (if perhaps a little intrusively) built-in behind the driver's seat. Inevitably, the air-cooling louvres also had to be repositioned, being cut into the body behind the rear wheel arches, while a new panel had to be generated to form the cab roof.

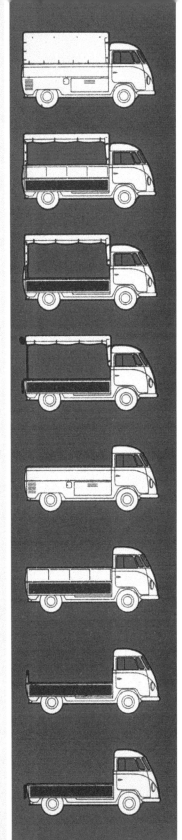

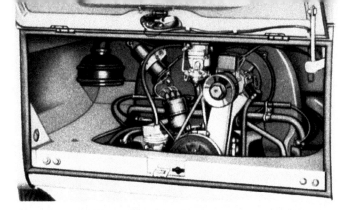

*Every possible inch of space
is utilized to increase load capacity.
In this tiny space
the Volkswagen engine develops its amazing power.*

"If desired, it can be delivered equipped with a weatherproof top and the necessary supports."

All the games of mechanical musical chairs so far described were crafted to create a Pick-up featuring a highly desirable full-length flat-bed of some 45ft². Hinged side flaps ensured that loads were not only easily accessible, but also unlikely to shoot off into the wild blue yonder when the vehicle accelerated away from whatever site it happened to be working on. To cap it all, the design team managed to create a weatherproof, top-hinged locker below the flat-bed, which not only gave owners a further 20ft² of space but also a convenient secure hideaway for items of value. Although only available at extra cost, a canvas top complete with 'tilt and hoops' ensured that, when necessary, all goods could be sheltered from the rain.

Here's what the marketing team had to say shortly after the Pick-up's launch: "If you buy a Volkswagen Pick-up, you will be delighted by its Volkswagen features. You will have a light truck that is a joy to drive and a joy to work with. It consumes so little fuel and costs so little in repairs – always less than you expect – that it is also a joy to pay for. Then just think of it, it is actually a double-

decker! The upper deck at normal level has 45ft² of floor space. The lower deck has 20ft² of floor space and is a closed compartment that can be locked. Do you know of any other ¾ ton pick-up truck with such features? ... The Volkswagen Pick-up is the ideal vehicle for speeding up your city delivery service. It will always be back from trips before you expect it. In the country you can drive it over the worst roads. The Volkswagen Pick-up will plough its way through road conditions that would stop the most powerful delivery truck mounted on a sedan chassis. It is the ideal truck for fast hauling."

If would-be purchasers believed all they read in the copywriters' text, perhaps it isn't surprising that 1606 Pick-ups were manufactured between its launch and the end of 1952. Further success followed and in the first full year of production 5741 Pick-ups were manufactured, making it just about as prolific as the Kombi in volume, with only the Panelvan out in front.

By the 1960s the copywriters had this to say: "The VW Pick-up is absolutely flat: no wheel housing is in the way. It's big: the platform is 8ft 6in long and 5ft 1in wide, giving an area of 45 square feet. Easy to load: both side and tailboards can be let down. It's robust: hardwood slats protect the corrugated platform and stop cargo from slipping. It has a large lockable compartment under the platform between the axles which

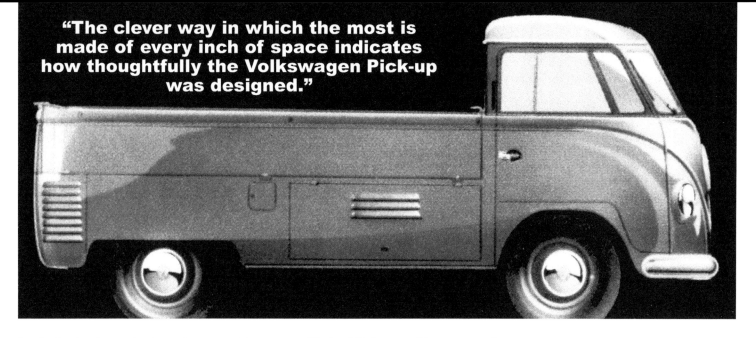

"The clever way in which the most is made of every inch of space indicates how thoughtfully the Volkswagen Pick-up was designed."

is absolutely dry and which gives you 20 square feet more load space."

Now note with care the suggested uses below for a Pick-up of the late 1950s, then look to the Ambulance and beyond and all will become clear in terms of Volkswagen's master plan.

"The VW Pick-up truck is particularly adaptable to different trade requirements. Here are some ideas:

• Mobile store and exhibition truck: brings your shop to your customers' doorstep.

• Glaziers' Pick-up – with one type of pane carrying frame.

• Pick-up with swivelling extension ladder – for street lamp servicing, tree trimming, checking overhead cables, bill-posting, fixing neon advertising and many other overhead jobs.

• Pick-up truck with jinker – for trailing loads: pipes, scaffolding, lumber, masts, boring rods, ladders ...

"... just a few of the thousand and one conversions that will meet your special needs just the way you want ..."

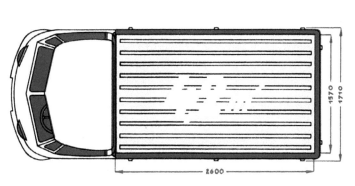

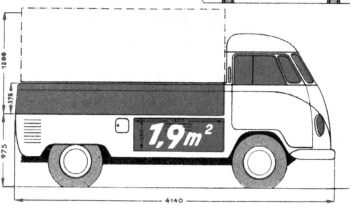

 VW Krankenwagen

"The Volkswagen Ambulance is the ideal means of conveyance for ill or injured persons."

What was Volkswagen playing at? Virtually every brochure issued for the better part of the fifties included space for Der VW Krankenwagen. Was this really such a mainstream vehicle that potential purchasers of Kombis, Microbuses and Panelvans needed to know that "every feature has been carefully planned to give the patients maximum comfort"?

As early as October 1950, the firm of Miesen, already well known for producing adaptations of vehicles for medical usage, was offering Kombi ambulances to hospitals. Just over a year later, on the 13th December 1951, Volkswagen launched its own standard factory model, designating it the Type 27 (21 being the Panelvan, 22 the Microbus, 23 the Kombi, 24 the Samba and so on). Perhaps it won't come as a great surprise to learn that production numbers trailed far behind those of any other model. In 1952, 481 Ambulances set off on their missions of mercy. The following year, 358 followed suit, while the last year of the decade resulted in the highest figure of all, a paltry 710, or 1.7 per cent of the Panelvan's triumphant score of 41,395 vehicles. Were Nordhoff and Volkswagen flogging the proverbial dead horse?

Here's what the copywriters had to say about the Ambulance in November 1953: "Every feature has been carefully planned to give the patients maximum comfort. Standard equipment for Volkswagen Ambulances includes two stretchers mounted at the same level on each side of the ambulance, an upholstered removable seat for carrying patients up and down narrow stairs, a further well-upholstered seat for patients and a folding-seat for the medical attendant next to the patients. The cabin seats the driver and two stretcher bearers."

To round the same brochure off, Volkswagen summarised the model range. Once again the Ambulance was granted an equal role to the rest of the players ...

"Type Details

VW Delivery Van with hinged double doors on the right (doors available on both sides at extra price).

VW Microbus accommodating 8 persons including the driver (also available at extra price with sun roof – Golde type).

VW Microbus Deluxe with Golde sun roof, all-round windows and side observation panels in roof.

VW Kombi with and without passenger seating accommodation, depending on whether intended for conveyance of passengers or goods (also available at extra price with sun roof – Golde type).

VW Pick-up with auxiliary load space under the main loading area (available at extra price with tilt and hoops).

VW Ambulance with two stretchers and additional seat for sitting casualty."

Special model calls for special equipment
Comprehension warning: read and digest carefully before turning the page!

Standard equipment for Der Krankenwagen (taken from 1961 VW Ambulance brochure).

Exterior: illuminated red cross roof sign; roof spotlight; reversing light; rear drop door, acts as a loading ramp for stretchers; retractable step under double side doors.

Interior: two stretchers (type DIN 13 025) with mattresses and pillows; grip-rail above each stretcher; communication buzzers from patients to driver; guide runners, sliding plates and locking devices for stretchers; one padded portable casualty chair; one padded seat with folding back; one emergency seat for attendant; fitted linoleum on floor and drop door; washable seamless cream leatherette linings for side panels and roof; cupboard and drawer for instruments, equipment and bandages, with space for portable first-aid cabinet below splint storage shelf; sliding windows and vent wings in cab; hinged left and right rear windows in ambulance

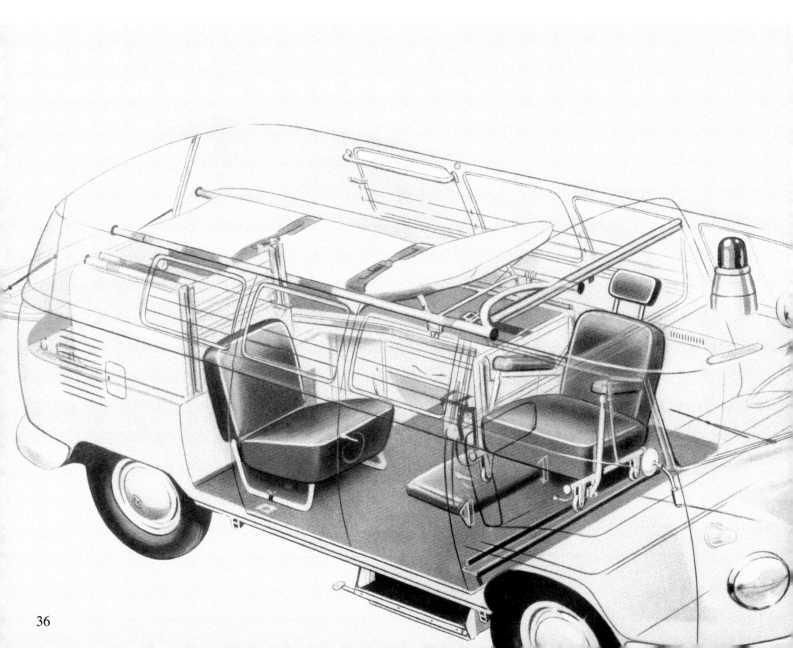

compartment; bright and dim adjustment of interior lighting, controlled from cab seat; fully adjustable heating for cab and ambulance compartment; heating can be restricted to cab alone; special adjustable ventilation with two electric ventilators (that still operate when vehicle is parked); fuel gauge; plug socket for inspection lamp.

Optional extras:

M150   Towing hooks front and rear. Runner extensions for ISO and US type stretchers. Retaining hooks and rubber straps for fixing a sled-type mining stretcher. Hinged pane on front wing door. Window guard rails on both wing doors. Driving cab lined with waterproof material throughout. Holders for kidney bowl, urine bottle, first-aid cabinet and axe. Windscreen washer. Second sun visor.

M151   Eberspächer stationary heater.
M152   Hinged extension flap on rear loading door.
M160   Eisemann flashing blue roof-light and Bosch two-tone horn.

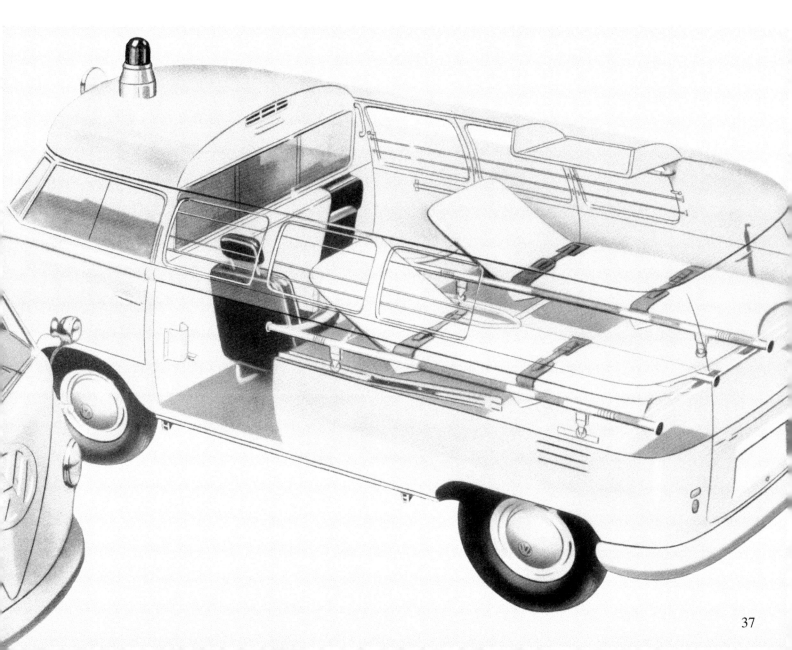

3. Factory options and special models

Mehrausstattung – 'M' codes/factory fitted options
Sonderausführungen – special models

*V*olkswagen quickly recognised that the Splittie could be an even greater success if it was available with numerous special body conversions, or if customers could select a whole host of factory fitted options to personalise the model of their choice. Including Der Krankenwagen and its 'M' code options in brochures let the world know that there was much more on offer than first appeared to be the case. Copywriters' comments on the versatility of the Pick-up reinforced it.

With a reproduction of a further page from the 1961 brochure, *The VW Ambulance* , here's a far from comprehensive list of some of the straightforward and downright obscure factory options available for Splitties:

MO25	Six pop-out windows and US bumpers (export)
MO26	Activated charcoal exhaust filter (USA, Canada, Japan)
MO28	Ambulance without stretcher
MO35	Reinforced sides for Pick-up
MO40	Speedometer with fuel gauge
MO53	Opening tailgate with window (until March 1955)
MO54	Full width Samba dashboard (until March 1955)
MO71	Second locker door (Pick-up)
MO77	88ah battery for Arctic climes
MO97	Rear bumper (until 1955)
M113	Opening windscreen panes (Safari) (export)
M130	Microbus Deluxe without sliding roof or roof windows
M161	Sliding-door Panelvan (one side)
M183	Walk-through cab Panelvan and Kombi RHD
M201	Pick-up with extended wooden platform
M225	VW Dealer breakdown/service vehicle
M515	Articulated unit
M535	Tachometer
M546	Flashing indicators on roof at the rear.

By the late 1950s, the brochure compilers and artists had included not just the Ambulance but also other vehicles that had been adapted for special uses. "These three special vehicles," spelled out the copywriter, "are built for utmost dependability. They are excellent examples of the versatility of VW Trucks and Station Wagons …".

By 1961, an amazing 130 options were on offer in addition to the set classics. Although some special models were equipped in-house, most were franchised out to special coachwork companies. One or two even became a part of the standard line-up of Splittie models, the as yet unmentioned Double Cab Pick-up being a prime example.

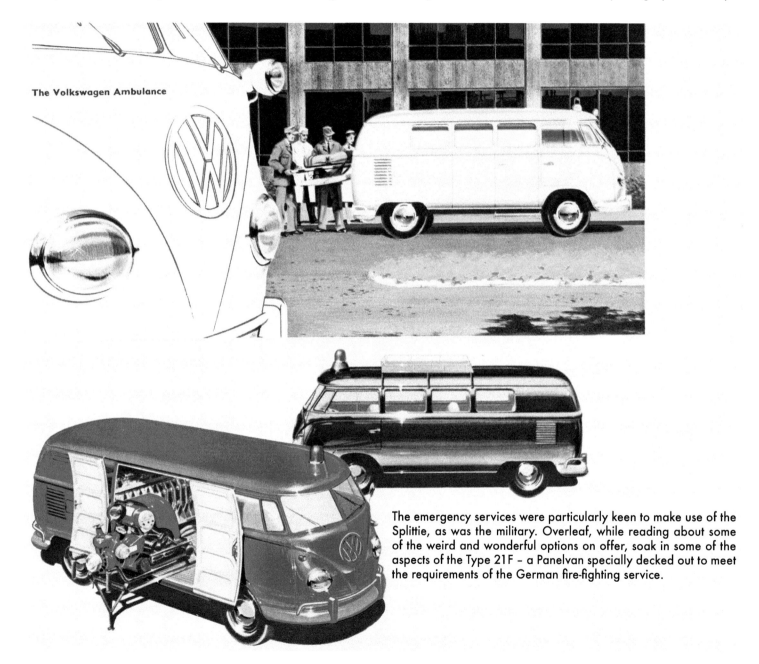

The Volkswagen Ambulance

The emergency services were particularly keen to make use of the Splittie, as was the military. Overleaf, while reading about some of the weird and wonderful options on offer, soak in some of the aspects of the Type 21F – a Panelvan specially decked out to meet the requirements of the German fire-fighting service.

From a straightforward mobile shop based on the Pick-up (SO13), to a glass-sided exhibition and display bus created out of a Panel van (SO19), specials came in all sorts of shapes and sizes. SO15 was a hydraulic tipper truck, while SO31 evolved around a Pick-up with a heating oil tank and dispenser pump. SO24 was a low loader. Arrangements could be made with an appropriate undertaker to be transported in a VW hearse, before climbing a ladder to the pearly gates utilising SO11, the ladder truck. The Dutch firm of Kemperink even developed a long-wheelbase version of the Pick-up, which, with a wheelbase of 3300mm compared to the normal 2400mm, afforded far more room to carry lengthy products than Volkswagen's standard offering. Still not satisfied, the same firm produced elongated Panelvans for biscuit manufacturers, a clothing company and even the army. Few but enthusiasts appreciate that SO22, originally the Westfalia Camping box, led directly to the numerous camping conversions covered in chapter four.

A typical example or two of the more unusual Splittie conversions on offer

Service Garages (South Eastern) Ltd, of Colchester, included in its range of conversions the 'SERV-ICE', the ice-cream van with "maximum storage and working space for the operator too". Launched in 1962, the company suggested that the VW 'SERV-ICE'

conversion could be carried out utilising the then recently launched high-roofed delivery van (see p66-7). Before itemising the full specification, Service Garages copywriter launched into a final

was "revolutionary in that the soft ice cream machine refrigerated cabinets and water heater etc ... [were] all driven from the vehicle's own power unit". Available with one of four options of ice cream making machine, or another brand a customer might care to specify, the Splittie featured either an elevating roof in Camper style, or a fixed fibreglass top, both offering headroom of 6ft 3in. Quick off the mark, Service Garages also mentioned that a

frenzy of selling points, noting that the 'SERV-ICE' was a "remarkable vehicle, priced at many hundreds of pounds lower than its competitors, with total running costs under half that which had been previously accepted as the minimum for this type of vehicle". With prices starting at £1550, such hyperbole was probably highly necessary, as the company's hard-ice model with an ICI Dri-Kold freezer system the total cost was a mere £885.

Chassis	15cwt Kombi details as per VW Transporter catalogue
Counter	30in ht. 53in length 15in width, with 9 sq ft shelving under
Sliding Window	19in x 14in for serving on road
Double Doors	Open to give full counter width for serving at fixed stands
Roof	The following alternatives can be supplied:- a) elevating b) fixed fibreglass c) high-roofed van
Conservators	Soft ice cream mix container – volume 7.4cuft, temperature maintained 32 – 35 degrees F automatically. Hard ice cream container – volume 3.9cuft, temperature maintained 0 degrees F automatically
Refrigeration gear	7,800 BTU at 30 degrees F Bitzer refrigerator unit driven in conjunction with Soft Ice Freezer by patented 'Service Conversion' gear from engine of vehicle. No electric motors, generators, auxiliary engines, control gear are employed and servicing virtually nil
Washing facilities	A hot and cold water supply is installed with draining board and washer bowl connected to 2½ gallon waste tank underneath in locker
Fluorescent lighting	Two fluorescent tubes are fitted as standard
Fresh air blower	is fitted giving adequate ventilation of vehicle under warmest operating conditions
All hours run counter	is fitted to engine for regulating servicing of engines

4. Splittie development

Volkswagen under Nordhoff was a very different regime in many respects to that of any of his successors. Speaking in 1948, shortly after his appointment as Director General, Nordhoff told the Volkswagen workforce that it was up to everyone at Wolfsburg, himself included, "to make this largest of all German motor car factories a decisive factor for Germany's peace-time economy". To achieve this goal fully, Volkswagen had to conquer the world. Exports were key; each product had to be of the highest quality. Although referring to the Beetle, the following Nordhoff declaration (made in the 1960s) summarises his philosophy and, by more than implication, Volkswagen's throughout the Director General's 20-year reign.

"In any sound design there are almost unlimited possibilities ... I see no sense in starting anew every few years, with the same teething troubles, making obsolete almost all of the past ... Offering people an honest value, a product of the highest quality, with low original cost and incomparable resale value, appealed more to me than being driven around by a bunch of hysterical stylists trying to sell people something they really do not want to have ..."

Although Nordhoff was pleased enough to introduce new models when the time was right, his unswerving belief in constantly improving existing products paid handsome dividends. While at face value it might appear that Volkswagen was too busy building the Splittie family of models, from the earliest of days the Transporter's specification was constantly under review. Over the page the subject is the first major revamp for the Splittie; similar in nature to the one the Beetle had received in the autumn of 1952 and would benefit from again in the summer of 1957. First however, to prove a point, here's a catalogue of some of the changes made to the Splittie during the time that new models were emerging, while there's also space devoted to the first engine upgrade which involved an increase of a mere 5bhp. However, with an original figure of just 25bhp, the boost was significant, especially in terms of acceleration times from rest.

30 m. p. g.

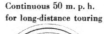

Continuous 50 m. p. h. for long-distance touring

Climbs up to 24.5 %

Selected specification changes 1950-53

16.6.50	Partition introduced between cab and load area.
11.9.50	Additional air vents (3) on upper rear panels (Panelvan).
11.11.50	Large rear-mounted VW roundel discontinued.
10.4.51	Aluminium VW badge replaced by same size sheet metal version.
20.7.51	Panelvan available with doors on both sides at extra cost.
1.9.52	Painted wiper arms now chrome-plated.
1.12.52	Pick-up rear window made of safety glass, previously merely thick glass.
2.1.53	Piano-hinge type quarter-lights replaced by pivoting type.
2.1.53	20 PCI Carb replaces 26 VFIS.
10.3.53	Synchromesh on 2nd, 3rd and 4th gears.
21.12.53	Backward style 80kph speedo replaced by conventional 100kph speedo.
21.12.53	30bhp engine replaces 25bhp version.

TYPE DETAILS VW DELIVERY VAN with hinged double doors on the right (doors available on both sides at extra price)
VW MICRO BUS accommodating 8 persons, including the driver (also available at extra price with sun roof — Golde type)
VW MICRO BUS DE LUXE with Golde sun roof, all-round windows and skylights

VW KOMBI with and wit on whether intended for at extra price with sun roo VW PICK-UP with auxili able at extra price with til VW AMBULANCE with 2

VOLKSWAGENWERK GMBH ·
WESTERN GERMANY

Specifications subject to change without notice

Autobahn-Dauergeschwindigkeit
80 km/h

Steigfähigkeit mit voller Last
bis 24 %

Müheloses Parker
auch auf kleinstem R

42

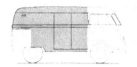 

Payload 1764 lbs. or
8 persons with luggage

Turning radius 19,7 ft.

Overall
and interior
dimensions
(in millimeters)

30bhp engine

Air-cooled, horizontally-opposed, four cylinders.

Capacity	1192cc.
Bore and stroke	77mm x 64mm.
Compression ratio	6.6:1 (6.1:1 Dec '53 – April '54 only).
Maximum power	30 bhp @ 3400rpm.
Maximum torque	76Nm @ 2000rpm.
Performance:	
Fuel consumption	30mpg.
Maximum & cruising speed	50mph.

Commercial Motor, April 2nd 1954

"There are few power units, for light commercial vehicles, that can compare with the efficient operation of the Volkswagen four-cylindered, horizontally-opposed petrol engine. In its entirety, the 15-cwt van is remarkable both in construction and performance ... it is speedy and economical, and well equipped, in its lowest ratio, to soar over the 1-in-4$\frac{1}{4}$ gradient of Succombs Hill with power to spare ... On a quiet level stretch of the road alongside the Thames, I found the acceleration rate to be from rest to 30mph 13.2 sec and to 40 mph 22.7 sec ... I acclaim the Volkswagen engine to be above average in its efficiency."

ating accommodation, depending
ssengers or goods (also available

der the main loading area (avail-

dditional seat for sitting casualty

LFSBURG

rights reserved · Printed in Germany

Mit 40 l Kraftstoff
420 km Fahrstrecke

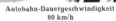

Autobahn-Dauergeschwindigkeit
80 km/h

Steigfähigkeit mit voller Last
bis 24 °/o

 5. Splittie developments: from 'barn door' to 'peaked cap' and beyond

Take time out to have a good look at a Splittie built before March 1955 and one of a later vintage. While there are significant differences at the rear of the two vehicles, it's to the front that most attention should be paid. Prior to March 1955 the bodywork was aesthetically simple, with the split screen only divided from the roof panel by a rain gutter. The roof itself culminated in one of the few extravagances afforded to the design, namely a stylish crease designed to flow with the line of the division between the split screens below. With effect from March 1955, the Splittie appeared to be wearing a peaked cap and most would probably agree that the re-design improved the overall look of the vehicle. More character possibly, definitely more clearly defined lines and less of an inference that the designers had skimped on the metal to produce a 'box on wheels'. Oddly, Herr Reuters failed to work his customary magic on the revised vehicle's appearance. Compare the heavy brow of the Splitties depicted here to the earlier examples of the artist's normally highly flattering work. Check out the flowing lines the artist generated for the Microbus as depicted on pages 20 and 21, plus the elegant look created for the pre-'55 models reproduced on the contents pages (4-5).

The purpose behind the donning of a peaked cap

*M*arch 1st 1955 saw the launch of the revised peak-cap Splittie. Since the Transporter's launch some five years earlier, more than a few criticisms had been levelled at Volkswagen regarding the lack of cab ventilation, with steamy windows proving almost inescapable on damp, dreary days, despite the provision of quarter-lights. The revised frontal appearance was not a stylist's whim, as this would hardly have been countenanced in the days of Nordhoff's Volkswagen. The peak had an entirely practical purpose, successfully solving the ventilation problem at a stroke.

Contained within the peak was an air-scoop complete with protective fine mesh gauze which was located as close as possible to the top of the windscreen, thus benefiting from maximum air turbulence as the Splittie trundled its way along the road. Within the cab, positioned on the underside of its roof, a collection and distribution box, manually controllable via a metal handle on the contraption's side, completed the alteration.

Anxious to spread the word to as many would-be purchasers as possible, Volkswagen went to great lengths to produce drawings illustrating the effectiveness of airflow in the Splittie. As the post March '55 Splittie also had a proper dashboard, whatever its status in the pack, coupled to a revised arrangements of heater outlets, artists were similarly employed to outline warm air circulation.

The copywriters found few problems explaining the arrangements in glowing terms and for that reason, if no other, the original captions to the reproduced images are retained here. Later in the 1950s, but still at a point before Volkswagen's marketing was set alight by a certain US advertising agency (p60-5), the write-up for the Microbus Deluxe was particularly expansive: "The intelligent design of the Deluxe Station Wagon is responsible for the many comforts and the desirable technical features of the driver compartment. Among them are the smooth upholstered seats, warm-air heating system, vent wings and sliding windows, padded sun visors, inside rear-view mirror, flexible grip in front of the passenger side and two-spoke steering wheel ..."

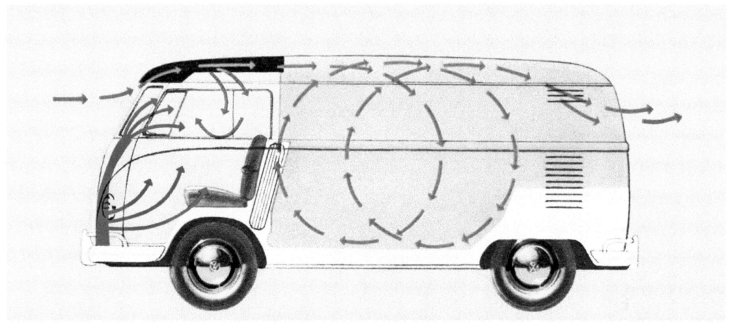

"The efficient heater, supplied as standard equipment, can be adjusted to suit individual requirements, allowing the driver to operate his vehicle even in extreme cold temperatures. The defroster and large windscreen wipers give him clear forward vision and prevent frosting of the window."

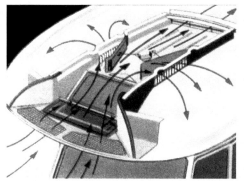

"With the vehicle in motion, the roof-mounted ventilation system is capable of renewing the total volume of air once every minute."

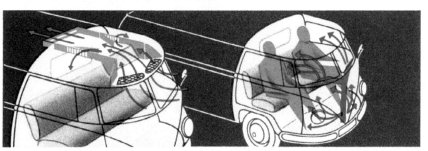

"Apart from the Volkswagen Transporter, there is no other vehicle in this range fitted with roof-mounted ventilation as standard equipment."

"Even in very low temperatures, the windscreen defroster, which is standard equipment, provides good visibility."

Now, why didn't we think of this before?

There was always something intrinsically primitive about the vast engine lid of the pre-March '55 Splittie. It might have acquired a fond nickname but in terms of practical or contemporary design the 'barn door' missed the plot. A precariously balanced fuel tank in a cavernous engine compartment, which dwarfed the tiny 25bhp, or early 30bhp, engine, appeared equally ludicrous.

As the illustrations reveal, in the March '55 shake-up such anachronistic features were swept away, making the Splittie a far more practical vehicle for a variety of owners. Perhaps it was that much-discussed Ambulance which incited the revolution. For the best part of four glorious years designers and bosses alike had stood and watched patients being loaded and unloaded through the ambulance's normal sized door. They had accepted and approved of the reduced size of the engine compartment and had even sanctioned the 'M' option of an opening hatch above the massive engine lid for the other members of the Splittie family. Why did it take so long for the penny to drop?

Despite access to the engine compartment now being slightly restricted, the abolition of the barn door literally opened a hatch on the Splittie for a whole new set of customers, including the individual depicted below loading a roll of linoleum or carpet into his Panelvan. As far as the engine went, the only adaptation

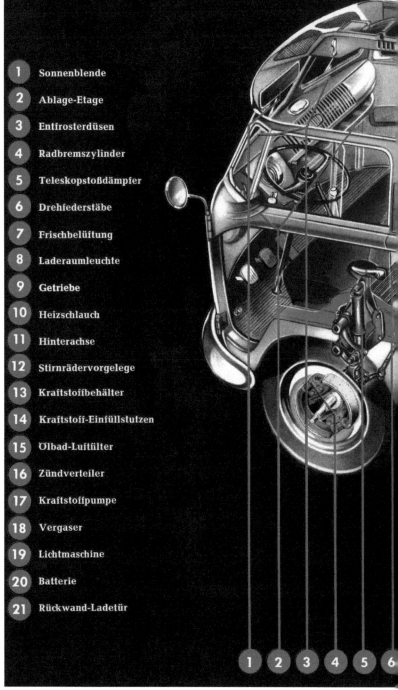

1	Sonnenblende
2	Ablage-Etage
3	Entfrosterdüsen
4	Radbremszylinder
5	Teleskopstoßdämpfer
6	Drehfederstäbe
7	Frischbelüftung
8	Laderaumleuchte
9	Getriebe
10	Heizschlauch
11	Hinterachse
12	Stirnrädervorgelege
13	Kraftstoffbehälter
14	Kraftstoff-Einfüllstutzen
15	Ölbad-Luftfilter
16	Zündverteiler
17	Kraftstoffpumpe
18	Vergaser
19	Lichtmaschine
20	Batterie
21	Rückwand-Ladetür

required to accommodate the new arrangements was to relocate the oil bath cleaner to the left of, rather than mount it above, the engine.

Filling up with fuel became easier too, as it was no longer necessary to go through the rigmarole of first opening the engine

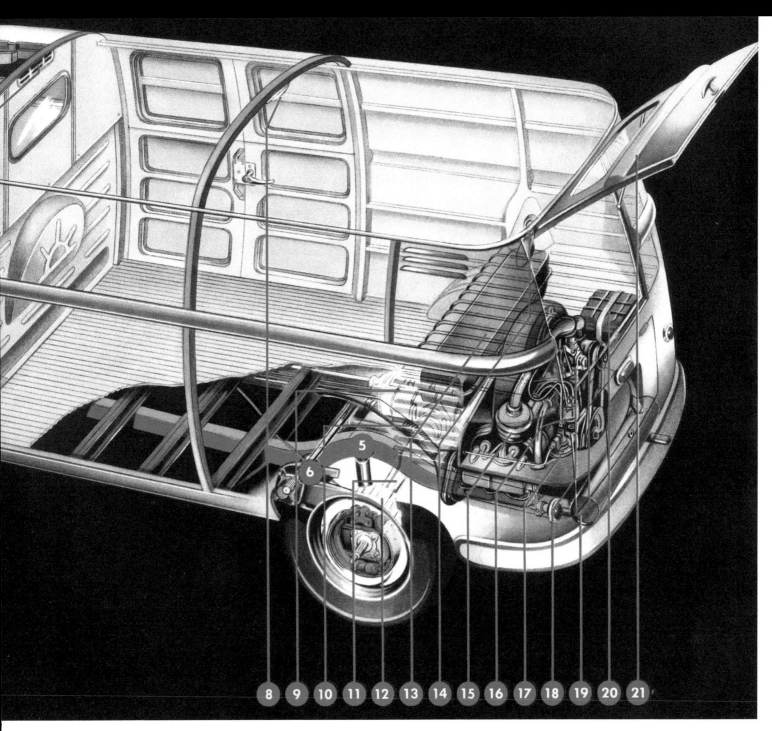

8 9 10 11 12 13 14 15 16 17 18 19 20 21

lid. A conventional flap on the body side, when opened with a suitably large key (christened the 'church key' by enthusiasts), revealed the fuel cap. As for the previously cumbersome spare wheel arrangement, a well was inserted behind the seats in the cab Pick-up-style and everybody was happy.

As if to stress a more modern approach to life, Volkswagen also reduced the size of the Splittie's wheel by one inch, down from 16in to 15in, while beefing up the tyre width from 5.50 x 16 to 6.40 x 15.

49

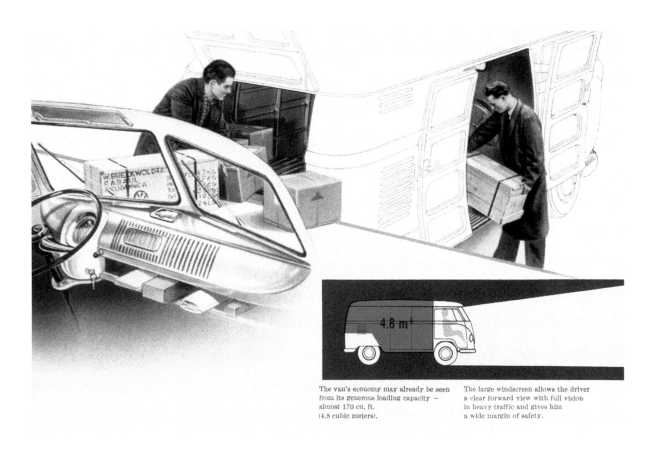

The van's economy may already be seen from its generous loading capacity — almost 170 cu. ft. (4.8 cubic meters).

The large windscreen allows the driver a clear forward view with full vision in heavy traffic and gives him a wide margin of safety.

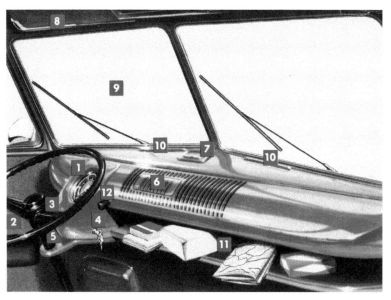

Dashing the full length

One other aspect of the new look Splittie deserves more than a passing mention. With the single exception of the super executive Samba, up to March 1955 all models had been endowed merely with a single pod binnacle to house what instruments there were. Now, although the new full-length, re-designed dashboard perhaps wasn't quite as attractive as that of the Deluxe models of old, it did encompass all models, bundling into the single VDO speedometer all the warning lights as well. In an age when smoking was the norm, prominence was given to an ashtray towards the centre of the dash while, in what many regarded as a retrograde step, the elegant three-spoke steering wheel was replaced by a more matter-of-fact two-prong affair.

Getting ahead in the USA

Less than a month after the March 1955 re-vamp, the Splittie was on the up once more, this time a privilege reserved for American and Canadian customers. Owing to a decided increase in traffic and the threat of impending legislation, Volkswagen dispensed with the services of the antiquated semaphore indicator, replacing it with a flashing bulb in a bullet-shaped casing. Sadly, it wasn't until June 1960 that models built for the European market followed suit. Almost inevitably, this later date proved to be only 13 months away from the time when the indicator design of Splitties in the USA was changed once more. The bullet indicators, having been deemed a potential danger to pedestrians, were replaced in July 1961 by a much flatter and larger arrangement, commonly known as the fish-eye lens. Europeans Splitties followed suite in 1963.

From the end of August 1958, US models received new two-tier bumpers, consisting of a substantial lower blade, tall overriders and a towel-rail-style upper bar. Introduced as a result of legislative pressure once more, and designed to offer extra bodywork protection in tight parking spaces against the higher bumpers of the average US wagon, American spec bumpers looked attractive and quickly became a popular accessory in other markets.

Not just 'getting ahead' but leaping along the production line!

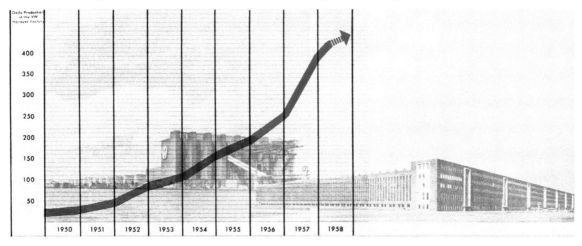

The first decade of production

1957

1950	8059
1951	12,003
1952	21,665
1953	28,417
1954	40,119
1955	49,907
1956	62,500
1957	91,983
1958	101,873
1959	121,453
1960	139,919

Panelvan	30,683
Kombi	23,495
Microbus	17,197
Pick-up	16,450
Samba	3514
Ambulance	644
Grand Total	91,983

As previously indicated the Panelvan started life as the only model. However, it retained pole position in the production stakes throughout the 1950s and beyond. By 1957 a popularity ranking had been well and truly established. A good year later a further member of the family (look to your right for a none-too-subtle clue) complicated the story.

Hopping over to Hanover

The decision to ship the Splittie out of Wolfsburg was taken by Nordhoff on January 24th 1955 and on March 9th 1956 the first vehicle, a Dove Blue Pick-up, emerged from the new production line. For several seasons, the copywriters took the opportunity to tell potential buyers that Volkswagen had built a factory especially for Splittie production ...

"The Volkswagen plant at Hanover went into production in 1956. Here, the finest automated machinery combined with traditional German craftsmanship to produce a precision-built, finely finished product ... The rise in production figures seen on the chart ... tells us why it was necessary to build this plant. Year after year, demand required greater production of all models. At present Hanover produces over 400 trucks daily. The big home plant at Wolfsburg now produces only sedans. Over 2000 roll of the assembly line there each day."

6. Twins! The Double Cab Pick-up

"Goods and people – if this is your transport problem, the six-passenger Pick-up will solve it."

Never known to miss a trick, Volkswagen had clearly watched the progress of the special model (SO16) Double Crew Cab Pick-up, manufactured by Binz with interest.

In October 1958, the single cab Pick-up became available with either a wooden platform or a wide bed, the latter increasing the load area from 45ft² to 55ft² and the overall width by some 13 inches. Both were initiated to satisfy the demands made by members of the building trade.

The logical next move came just one month later, when Volkswagen announced its own Double Cab Pick-up, bestowing upon it the model designations 265 and 267, dependent on the location, left or right, of the rear cab door, plus 268 for the RHD, left cab door version. Clearly, Volkswagen was aware of the sales figures for the Binz, after all it provided the single cab

models on which the special was moulded, and decided that the reasonably extensive re-tooling required was worth the time and the effort. Apart from the need for a larger roof panel, a rear cab side door had to be fabricated, as had both a shorter bed and a revised cab. Gone was that much vaunted dry-weather lower storage area, although there was room for some articles below the new rear bench seat.

The copywriters set to work to sell the additional product, with one early hit coming in the shape of the following: "You take half a Kombi and half a Pick-up, put them together and presto, you have a completely different type of utility vehicle with many special, nay unique, advantages ..."

By 1961 the US team could summarise the Double Cab Pick-up with such ease that there seems little point in doing anything more than reproducing its story here: "The Double Cab Pick-up can do the job of a pick-up truck or a sedan or both. The heated and ventilated double cabin seats five comfortably. The cargo deck has a flat-bed load area of 30ft² and can carry a 1000lb payload. It has hinged sides and tail gate. Bows and tarpaulin are optional, giving 108ft³ of enclosed space behind the cab. The rear seat and tool chest beneath it can be removed and the 65ft³ of space used for cargo. Ideal for carrying workmen and all their supplies, the Double Cab Pick-up is recommended especially to public utilities, contractors, farmers and landscape gardeners. It will transport the driver and 1543lb of cargo, two people and 1400lb of cargo, or five people plus 826lb – and it will do it efficiently and economically."

Goods and people —
if this is your transport problem,
the six-passenger Pick-up will solve it.

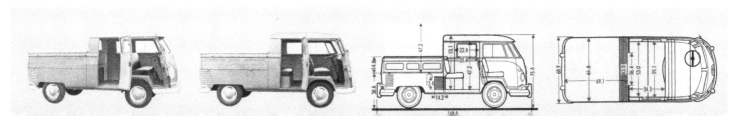

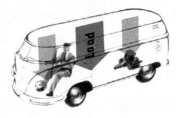
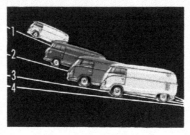

7. Not one, but two new engines

Where the Beetle had trodden, the Splittie had followed ... until now that is!

The eagle-eyed will have already spotted a flaw in the above statement – the Splittie never bumbled to a halt with the rather leisurely cable brakes bestowed on all pre-April 1950 Beetles. However, with that anomaly overlooked, it wasn't until 1959 that the situation changed. For a few years there had been increasing comment that the old 30bhp engine was somewhat underpowered for the task it had to perform. Independent tuning firms set to work to rectify this issue but, inevitably, packages including twin carbs, larger cylinder barrels and pistons, to name but two departures, didn't come cheap. Take-up levels were low, the moaners preferring to continue in the same vein.

Nordhoff bowed to pressure and, from May 19th 1959, the Splittie received a new engine – one that was no more powerful than its predecessor! Outwardly distinguishable from both the old 30bhp and 25bhp units by its detachable alloy dynamo pedestal, compared to the single cast of the old unit, the new engine demonstrated a number of advantages in terms of efficiency over its predecessor. Although both bore and stroke remained the same, the compression ratio

was raised slightly. The crankcase halves were much stronger, as were the retaining studs and bolts used to hold them together. A sturdier crankshaft replaced the version that had been prone to failure when mileage was high and full revs had been employed most of the time. The cylinder barrels were placed slightly further apart, which had the effect of improving cooling and valve diameters were increased. Thanks to the speed of the cooling fan having been reduced, the new engine appeared to be quieter.

The new engine might have been more efficient but it did little overall to satisfy demand for more power, and some thirteen months later, on June 1st 1960, Volkswagen at last announced that the Splittie was to have a little more 'oomph', with the number of horses rising from 30 to 34! Out went the long-serving Solex 28PCI carb, to be replaced with the new 28PICT version. The compression ratio was raised to 7.0:1 and the new maximum bhp was achieved at 3600rpm. Additionally, the ratio of the reduction gears in the axle hubs was altered from 1.4:1 to 1.39:1. The net result was insignificant in terms of the top speed,

but the Splittie was a far livelier beast, with better acceleration, improved performance through the gears and much smoother running. The critics were silenced, at least temporarily, despite the fact that rival manufacturers were now offering vehicles with engines developing double the brake horse power of the Splittie.

The September 1961 issue of *Car Life* compared a Splittie, Ford Econoline and Chevrolet Greenbier, noting their respective horse power ratings (US SAE applicable). While the Splittie rolled in at 40, the Greenbrier clocked up 80 and the Ford headed the ratings at 85. Although the Volkswagen's 1192cc engine might have been "hard pressed to move the 2310lb vehicle", it could cover "the quarter mile acceleration test as fast as the Greenbrier with its Powerglide automatic transmission". Top speed, the reviewer claimed, "is just at 60mph, which can be maintained for hours without harm. Long uphill grades, however, can be a bit annoying, although the VW is as nimble as a chamois on twisty mountain roads." Turning to the Ford, 'the long gap between the 2nd and top ratios could mean that you're not going to pass the VW going up that long grade"', while it "should get slightly better mileage than the Greenbrier, less than the VW ... As for noise levels inside the vehicles, we prefer the rear mounted engines ..." With reviews such as this hitting the motoring press, Nordhoff was fully justified in his conservative actions, wasn't he?

VOLKSWAGENWERK GMBH · WOLFSBURG · GERMA

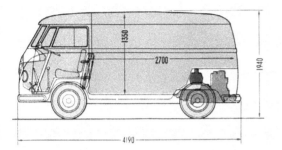

Dimensions in millimetres

by Nordwest-Druck, Hamburg. The right is reserved to alter specifications at any time without notice.

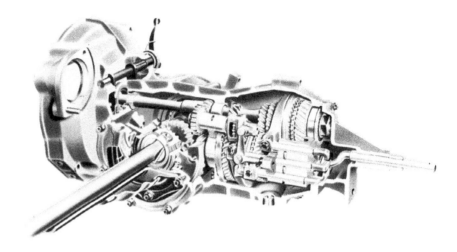

8. Promoting the product

Vehicles which were meant to be seen ... and the odd one that wasn't!

VWs starting on Safari to Serengeti Park.

Let's be bluntly honest: the turgid and contrived text of the 1950s copywriter would be as appealing to today's would-be Volkswagen purchasers as the addendums to legal documents. Nevertheless, unless the science of marketing, advertising and promotion is bunk, and the success of a product is entirely due to other factors, the copywriters' words and Reuters' artwork served Volkswagen well throughout the

1950s. Thanks to one of Nordhoff's protégés, soon all this would change and Volkswagen products would be promoted in the most dynamic of fashions, initially in America and then, slowly but surely, across just about every market imaginable.

The very first Splittie sold (on March 8th 1950) was delivered in primer to Autohaus Fleischhauer in Cologne. Its client was the 4711 Perfume Company, whose intention it was to have the vehicle customised using its brand colours and company logo. During 1950, close on 43 per cent of Panelvans

would leave Wolfsburg wearing nothing more than coats of primer for the selfsame reason. Businesses wished to personalise the product, making use of the large and relatively flat panels to advertise their services or wares. Even 23 per cent of the Kombis manufactured were despatched to customers in a similar state, while 18 per cent of the then top-of-the-range Microbus were accounted for in their 'underwear'. Clearly, here was a major selling point of the new range. The marketers were charged with advertising the fact.

Artists duly concocted the most extravagant of patterns and designs to decorate the Splittie at least on paper, as depicted below. Sufficient care was also taken to photograph some of the vehicles already on the road, which sported the liveries of their companies. Then, in the high-summer of 1952, a dedicated brochure under the title *Wer Fährt VW Transporter*, which translates as *Who drives a VW Transporter* , was meticulously put together featuring the full story of liveried Splitties. Once established, the theme arose again and again, as the Splitties adorned with logos depicted overleaf testify. Sadly, the copywriter's text did little justice to the concept.

1953 – "The Volkswagen Delivery Van has large smooth panels ideal for advertising. They can be made into travelling signboards that are the cheapest but most effective advertising you can give your firm."

1953 – "Cost-conscious businessmen have found out that billboard space equal in size to the advertising area on the Volkswagen Delivery Van costs more during one year than the entire Volkswagen. That is why they are so anxious to utilise both the large sides and the top of the vehicle for impressive and effective publicity."

Lots of useful space

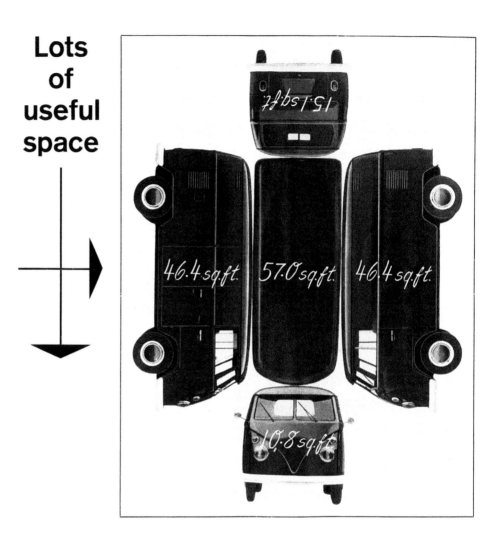

"Painted to catch the eye ..."

Whether through stencil techniques or by transfers, Buses were liberally dosed with promotional material throughout the Splittie era. By the mid-1960s the copywriters' story was altogether slicker: "Advertising on a VW Commercial must be attractive, must draw attention to itself, must contain good arguments, must pass on information and make the reader act on its suggestion. This could be done by skilful use of either colour or

lettering or a combination of both."
"[Each] VW fleet owned by a number of famous brand names ... run several hundred VW Commercials ... and these travel all over West Germany, to and around West Berlin and are at one and the same time 'Hoardings on Wheels' for their ... contents."
"[There is proof] that you do a lot of advertising around town by using a VW Commercial – virtually for nothing. For the VW goes and goes anyway. It is an ideal medium for advertising."

Doyle Dane Bernbach ... new decade, new style

In 1954 Carl Hahn joined Volkswagen, initially as Heinz Nordhoff's personal assistant. Later he was to join the export department's sales promotion operation. By 1959, he had been offered, and had accepted, the position of head of VW of America. Although sales of both the Beetle and the Splittie were buoyant, Hahn was aware that US manufacturers were ready to fight back, stemming the flow of all foreign vehicles, including Volkswagens. In a pre-emptive defence move, Hahn decided to advertise the product range, something that had been thought largely unnecessary previously. In need of an agency, Hahn met more than 4000 admen, taking three months to find his ideal. DDB had been formed just 10 years earlier, a partnership involving Bill Bernbach, Ned Doyle and Mac Dane. DDB was determined to turn traditional car advertising on its head. Hahn was impressed and, though he commissioned the firm of Fuller, Smith and Ross (a firm that had previously specialised in industrial advertising) to cover the Splittie, within 12 months DDB had secured all Volkswagen's advertising. The Beetle and now the Splittie were in its care.

WHICH IS
THE SHAPE OF TRUCKS
TO COME?

Volkswagen, the truck that picks up more for less

DDB stripped away the accepted norms of 1950s car advertising. Realistic and often stark images replaced both flattering artwork and carefully concocted photography. Lens distortion disappeared overnight. The suave drivers of the past were as redundant as the shapely, elegant females who had swooned in admiration at the most basic of models. DDB's copywriter, Julian Koenig, dismissed the self-congratulatory and frankly dull words of days gone by that had filled the pages before his arrival. DDB's self-deprecating style treated readers as intelligent beings, galvanising their minds as no advertising had done before. Honesty of an almost disarming nature, coupled with wit and wisdom, was rewarded by an almost immediate boost in sales. As a tribute to the ingenuity of DDB's campaign, turn the page to find the only examples of brochures reproduced exactly as they were first issued, not a word of text amended, not a full stop dislodged.

What is it?

Glad you asked

It's a Volkswagen Station Wagon.

Don't pity the poor thing; it can take it.

It can carry nearly a ton of anything you can afford to buy.

Or 8 people (plus luggage) if you want to get practical about it.

And there's more than one practical consideration.

It will take you about 24 miles on a gallon of regular gas.

It won't take any water or anti-freeze at all; the engine is air-cooled.

And even though it carries almost twice as much as regular wagons, it takes 4 feet less to park.

What's in the package?

8 pairs of skis, the complete works of Dickens, 98 lbs. of frozen spinach, a hutch used by Grover Cleveland, 80 Hollywood High gym sweaters, a suit of armor, and a full sized reproduction of the Winged Victory of Samothrace.

That's about the size of it.

That special paint job is to make it perfectly clear that our Station Wagon is only 9 inches longer than our Sedan.

Yet it carries almost a ton of anything you like. (About twice as much as you can get into wagons that are 4 feet longer.)

Or eight solid citizens, with luggage.

Or countless kids, with kid stuff.

The things you never think about are worth thinking about, too.

You never worry about freezing or boiling; the rear engine is air-cooled.

You can expect about 24 miles per gallon and about 35,000 miles on your tires.

And you can forget about going out of style next year; next year's model will look the same.

The Volkswagen Station Wagon comes in red and white or grey and white or green and white.

And you won't ever have to go around painting sedans on it to show how small it is.

Just park.

Can you spot the difference?

With the arrival of DDB to promote the product, plus the new 34bhp engine and an all-synchromesh box to liven up the Splittie's performance, it was clear that the 1960s were going to be very different to the '50s. The brochure cover produced above is clearly a product of the passing era, even though it was released in 1961. Compare the style with that of the 1962 edition reproduced opposite. The way ahead was clear, both with the Splittie and the Beetle;

Reuters had produced his last illustration for Volkswagen. Although by 1960 the Splittie was in its eleventh year of production, there was no thought of replacing it. Production statistics confirm that the 1960s saw continued levels of growth, while yet another variation on the theme had yet to see the light of day when the decade dawned. Motoring journalists were happy. The golden age, which had emerged in the 1950s, was set fair to continue.

Splittie production figures 1960-66

151,218	1960
168,600	1961
180,337	1962
189,294	1963
200,325	1964
189,876	1965
191,373	1966

You can

with a Volkswagen Station Wagon

"Meet the Volkswagen Truck – As the Volkswagen Sedan started a trend toward the family economy car, the VW Truck pioneered economical transportation for the businessman. In this truck, economy is not a catchword but an engineering ideal. There is both economy of line in its styling and economy of motion in its performance. The VW Truck is only nine inches longer than the VW Sedan and correspondingly agile; yet it carries more than three-quarters of a ton. It's superbly crafted, yet tough as they come. The VW Truck is advanced, yet not experimental: 178 improvements have been made over the past 12 years. In fact, it has been tested and approved by more than 125,000 tough-minded businessmen. They have found it is the sensible means for carrying loads under a ton. We think you will, too."

"The Anatomy of a Volkswagen – How to design a truck which will carry a big load yet be light and manoeuvrable,

that will be tough enough to do the job, yet economical to run and maintain, that will provide comfort for the driver and yet make loading and unloading efficient? Eliminate dead weight and you solve your problems with a new idea in truck design. Cool the engine with air: no water, no radiator. Use magnesium-aluminium alloys, the lightest made today. Make the body of unitised construction: no bolts, 13,000 spot-welds. Put the engine in the rear: no heavy driveshaft. Result: 1600lb. Less dead weight. An engine in the rear will balance your truck and provide superior traction (when others are stuck in mud, sand or snow, you go). To design an economy truck, start with a new idea."

Two extracts from *Meet the Volkswagen Truck* – VW of America, 1961.

9. A last addition to the family

What was to prove to be the final addition to the official Splittie range, the high-roof, or high top Panelvan, drifted onto the scene in the early autumn of 1961 for the '62 model year. In specification terms, the only difference between the new model and the standard Panelvan was straightforward, the high-roof had extended body panels and taller side doors.

While the louvres for the load compartment were raised, continuing to be as close to the roof panel as possible, the standard Panelvan tailgate was retained. Whereas the standard Panelvan stood 1925mm (75.8in) tall, the new model clocked in at 2285mm (90in).

Meet the High-Roofed Delivery Van

Inevitably, as the high-roof was constructed entirely out of steel, it suffered a weight penalty tipping the scales up to 1110kg (2447lb) compared to the Panelvan at 1070kg (2359lb). Volkswagen was quick to impose a slight payload penalty, amounting to 40kg, or less than two standard bags of potatoes! Not that it really mattered anyway, as the vehicle found popularity with members of the clothing trade, the German Post Office and glaziers, all of whom tended to carry lighter rather than heavier items. "It's even easier to load and unload," boasted an exuberant copywriter, "the double wing doors are larger still. It has more load space, of course. Instead of 170ft³, you have 212ft³ of space in the load compartment. Goods can be arranged neatly. Plenty of room to work in means that you can stand up while inside the load compartment."

The paper chase

Volkswagen produced literally dozens and dozens of brochures to promote the Splittie and other members of the family during the 'sixties, the marketing men frequently tweaking both their designs and text. The red Splittie above

adorned the cover of a portrait-style brochure printed in 1963 (a landscape version was also available), while the subtly improved offering featuring a classic Dove Blue Splittie, complete with packing crates overflowing with character and detail, was printed in 1965.

25% more horsepower now available

10. Those final classic years

With the launch of a larger VW saloon, the VW 1500, in the autumn of 1961, Volkswagen had a ready-made and more powerful engine available to slip into the Splittie. While nobody was really complaining loudly, if at all, Nordhoff had kept an eagle eye on the competition. Everywhere, and particularly in the USA, manufacturers were avidly playing the power game. Thus it came to pass that from January 7th 1963, American models received the 1500 engine, while by March it was an option for other markets providing the Splittie in question was of a passenger carrying nature. In August, for the '64 model year, even the worker bee Splitties were available with the 'Fifteen', which inevitably led to a decline in 1200 sales, followed by its deletion from the range in October 1965.

Although technically the 1500 was little more than a bored out 1200 (OK – different crankshaft, crankcase, pistons and barrels), it was deemed by many to be the best air-cooled engine Volkswagen ever produced.

Boosting the horses – the Fifteen

An increased bore and stroke of 83mm x 69mm raised capacity to 1493cc, while the compression ratio was higher at 7.5:1, resulting in an 8bhp increase over that of the 1200.

In Volkswagen's truly conservative style, a new top speed of 65mph was quoted, while the extra power resulted in the payload being lifted from 750 to 1000kg.

When reports reached Nordhoff's ears of people travelling at speeds in excess of 75mph in their 1500-powered Splitties, alarm bells sounded. Volkswagen did not wish to be sued by victims of fully laden Panelvans crashing out of control at such high speeds. As a result, from August 1964 all Fifteens were fitted with a carburettor throttle governor. Inevitably, this device made overtaking trickier and resulted in a lack of power when negotiating steeper hills. Fortunately, with the fitting of a more efficient carburettor (a 28 PICT-1) in August 1965, and an increase in the size of the inlet and outlet valve diameters, the Fifteen could breathe more easily. Overall bhp went up by two to 44 and everybody was happy.

"Why make the VW Commercial's rear door and window even bigger?"

The pattern of annual upgrades to coincide with the new model year, which kicked in after Volkswagen's summer holiday period at the end of July, had become firmly established by the 1960s, although changes did occur at other times, witness the appearance of the 1500 engine.

In August 1963, not only did fish-eye indicators become universal, having previously been restricted to the US market, but also the reduction gears were modified and the hubcaps no longer benefited from a painted logo at their centres. The biggest change however was a substantial

increase in the size of the tailgate and its inset window, helping, as the copywriter was quick to point out, "you to see better what is going on behind". Sadly, one model in the range lost out: the Samba of 23-window fame was no more, as clearly the wraparound rear quarter panes could no longer be squeezed into position. From this point onwards the Samba was down to just 21 windows, its appearance altered and its modern day value slightly diminished. Hey ho!

Opting for the options ...

Flick through the pages of any brochure promoting the Splittie in the mid-1960s and there's an emphasis on variety. Apart from the normal Panelvan then, browsers could expect to be confronted with "the VW Delivery Van with sliding doors", the High-Roof Delivery Van (which you'd come to expect), the Pick-up, the Pick-up "with enlarged platform", "Zeer praktish, de VW met dubbele kabine" (c/o Pon's Automobielhandel N V), the Kombi and, if you were lucky enough, other once rarely referred to options.

Consider the dilemma facing the copywriter: how to get the message across without complicating the story beyond comprehension? The extract quoted opposite devoted to the intricacies of door arrangements and the Panelvan is on the limit!

Because there's more to opt for!

"It has two large doors in the cab. It has large double wing doors – four feet by four feet – on the left side of the body. It also has (on request) large double wing doors on the right hand side. There is another large door in the rear – 29 inches high and 48 inches wide – opens upwards and remains in position. The standard VW Delivery Van has only the one double wing door on the left side plus the rear door. Enough for most delivery requirements. On the other hand, some businessmen prefer wing doors on both sides (available at extra charge), so that they can load and unload from either side. Likewise, you can also have one sliding door or two (at extra charge). You pay a little more for sliding door(s) but they make loading easier sometimes. Sliding doors don't open outwards, so in tight places, you have more room to load or unload."

From smaller wheels to ...

To the end of Splittie production, Volkswagen continued to improve the product, with one of the most useful of all advances being reserved for the final model year. Surprisingly little play was made of the fact that from August 1966 all Splitties benefited from the introduction of 12-volt electrics (for the previous few years this luxury had been an optional extra (M620), but the extra expense involved had deterred all but the most resolute). The advantages over the old system could be seen in Splitties that started easily however cold the weather was, while night-time driving was no longer an anxious experience of groping about by candlepower. Perhaps on reflection, Volkswagen considered it wise to play down the move to 12-volts as, with the exception of models destined for the USA, the Beetle clung onto its 6-volt system for another year. Additionally, how could you photograph the advantages? The subtlety of selecting a Double Cab Pick-up whose owners are clearly working on some sort of overhead cabling system as reproduced here, would undoubtedly have been lost on many brochure readers.

... 12-volt electrics to brighten up your day

Other amendments included the apparently unusual decision to reduce the size of the wheels to 14in rather than use the customary 15in ones, which still prevailed not only on the Beetle, but also the VW 1500 and, of course, the Karmann Ghia. This update came in August 1963, as did the safety conscious move to amend the nine outward facing vents to ten, which profiled inwards. In August 1965, the flasher switch was moved from its antiquated floor-mounted position to the steering column, while the Pick-up gained a larger window at the rear of its cab. Even the hallmark church key was phased out a year later when a finger pull was introduced to open the fuel filler flap.

VW Double Cab Pick-up with bows and tarpaulin

Our School Bus

SAFELY TO SCHOOL

The Volkswagen that had everything to write home about!

The Splittie bowed out at the end of the '67 model year. Between its launch in March 1950 and the day in July 1967 when the vehicle bearing chassis number 217 148 459 came off the production line, 1,833,000 Splitties had been built at either Hanover or Wolfsburg, while additional production occurred in Brazil, South Africa and Australia. Like the Beetle, the Splittie was exported to well over 100 countries across the world, while some satellite operations were responsible for the assembly of knock-down-kits.

Today the Splittie is probably loved even more than when it was in production, if that is possible. The prices paid for Concours condition examples have escalated to such an extent that now it is more than feasible to purchase a brand-new, top-of-the-range, medium-sized saloon for less money than Nordhoff's humble box on wheels. From School Bus to Microbus Deluxe, Pick-up to Krankenwagen, the Splittie was a classic then and remains so today.

 1. Introducing the all-new 'updated' Bay

"The new VW Commercial has had a face-lift. Its looks have been improved. But that's not all."

To the casual observer, without any pre-knowledge of the Volkswagen story, publicity material released in the summer of 1967 might suggest that two new models had been announced within days of each other; one being 'The New Beetle', the other 'The New VW Commercial'. The reality, of course, was somewhat different. Whereas the saloon had received a safety-first makeover, with re-designed wings to accommodate vertically positioned headlamps up front, plus a stubbier bonnet and engine lid to make way for sturdier box-section bumpers and little else, the Transporter was genuinely new.

Conceived in 1964, when Splittie sales were undoubtedly booming, the concept behind the Bay should have killed the notion that Nordhoff was incapable of axing a product. After all, here was the first genuine replacement model in the growing family of Volkswagens. However, the fallacy of Nordhoff's intransigence remained more or less intact and, despite the occasional headline, the marketing men were of little help. For, although that word 'new' might appear, it was invariably accompanied by contradictory phrases. Witness, for example, this offering written by an eager-to-please copywriter in the summer of 1967: "The new VW Commercial has had a face-lift. Its looks have been improved." A US brochure of identical vintage, while crammed with carefully crafted words in the best tradition of advertising gurus Doyle Dane Bernbach, failed to make any mention of the word 'new' on its cover. "The Volkswagen family of trucks ... come on inside and meet them. You might want to take one into your business" was the bland message, while elsewhere statements such as "standard equipment ... [there's] a sliding door (it used to cost extra too)", hardly bawled the message of a new Transporter from the rooftops.

For people who like to see where they are going, who want to view the distant panoramas ... the Bay

Clearly and instantly recognisable as a Volkswagen in the tradition of its predecessor, the designers had nevertheless started with a blank sheet of paper when they huddled together for the first time to give birth to the Bay. That for many years the second generation Transporter has been known as 'the Bay', is evidence enough of the vehicle's most noticeable asset – its panoramic windscreen. Although only 27 per cent larger than the combined total of the two panes in the Splittie, the fact that the screen was noticeably curved, indeed had 'wraparound' qualities, made it appear considerably more modern and airy.

Long rectangular windows in the passenger carrying models instead of the more numerous but smaller and nearer-to-square windows in the Splittie had the same sleek effect, while the introduction of an air-grille below the windscreen was not only a highly modern innovation, but also gave character to what could have been a much blander and flatter frontal appearance. The decision to include a prominent and sizeable VW roundel on the Bay's front was one of genius, as the Splittie legend lived on through this symbol of honest-values and reliability.

"The full-width, curved windscreen ... means good visibility and plenty of light inside ... The two-speed windscreen wipers have large blades ... Generous exterior mirrors project on each side giving a really wide rear view ... The flashing indicators up front are new. But this isn't just for art's sake. They're larger too. Which makes them even easier to see than before." Launch text, 1967.

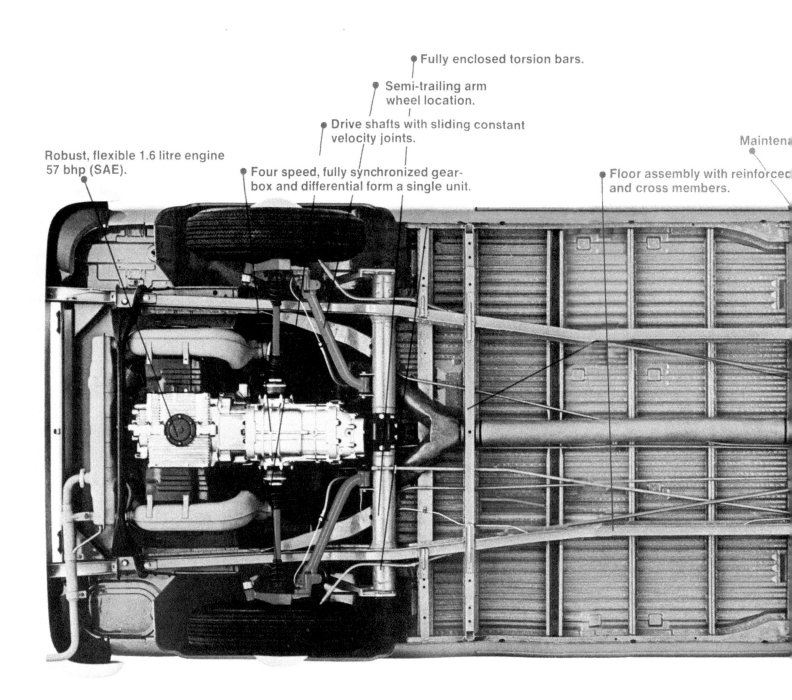

Fully enclosed torsion bars.

Semi-trailing arm
wheel location.

Drive shafts with sliding constant
velocity joints.

Robust, flexible 1.6 litre engine
57 bhp (SAE).

Four speed, fully synchronized gearbox and differential form a single unit.

Maintena

Floor assembly with reinforced
and cross members.

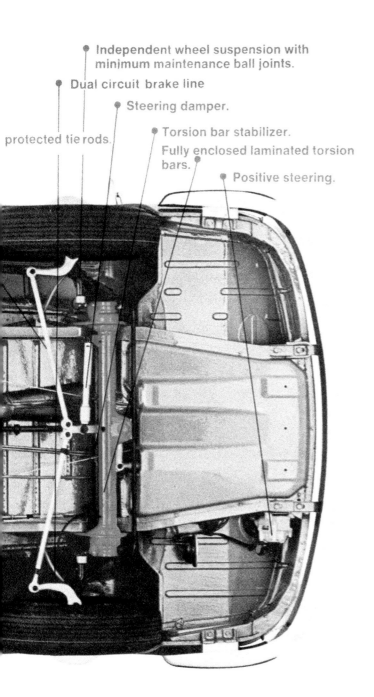

Independent wheel suspension with minimum maintenance ball joints.

Dual circuit brake line

Steering damper.

protected tie rods.

Torsion bar stabilizer.

Fully enclosed laminated torsion bars.

Positive steering.

Beef behind the Bay?

Although the Bay was over five inches longer than the Splittie (Splittie 168.5in/4280mm, Bay 174in/4420mm), it was constructed on the same principles. Two longitudinal members formed the backbone of the chassis frame, while cross-members and outriggers reinforced the sills and further flung bodywork. As clearly shown below, the longitudinal members ran the full length of the vehicle, merely lifting where they encountered both the rear and front suspension units. As the frame was integrated into the underbody, just as with the Splittie, here was a unitary chassis-cum-body.

Suspension remained in the finest Volkswagen tradition, employing the independent torsion bar system in a beefed-up form. The copywriters spoke of a smoother ride, for the much-improved driveshafts were fitted with constant velocity joints, unlike the Splittie's swinging-axle system. However, the advance in road holding was attributable more to an increase in track over the older model.

"It has a double-joint rear axle (usually only found in fast, upper price bracket passenger cars). The track has been widened considerably, both front and rear. The springing has been completely redesigned. Result? Road holding that would put many a passenger car to shame."

Weighing in at 2174kg, the Bay in delivery van form was some 104kg heavier than the equivalent Splittie (2070kg)! A more powerful engine was clearly needed, if VW had any chance of keeping up with rival manufacturers in its most important export market, the USA. The typically cautious, conservative solution was to increase the size from 1493cc to 1584cc. With a bore and stroke of 85.5mm x 69.0mm, the 1600 produced a maximum of 47bhp at 4400rpm (57bhp SAE). As the top and cruising speed remained the same at 65mph, the US copywriters came up with a cunning plan ...

"This year's engine is stronger. A little more horsepower and a lot more torque. (Not to make the truck go faster. But just so it doesn't have to work so hard.)" Of course air-cooled reliability also had to be stressed. "They never use anti-freeze. Since the Volkswagen engine is air-cooled, there's nothing to freeze. Or boil over. Or coolant to run out of. So quite apart from saving you money, our air-cooled engine means you won't wind up pulled over to the side of the road, steaming on a hot day. Or stuck with a cracked radiator in the middle of winter."

The Volkswagen 'ready-made' family of trucks

Unlike the Splittie, which had emerged in its various guises over the years, it was expected that Volkswagen would offer all variants of 'the box that comes with the good looks' from day one, something it duly proceeded to do. As a result, publicity shots which included examples of the Panelvan, the Pick-up – both in Single and Double Cab form, the Kombi, the Microbus and Microbus Deluxe soon appeared.

Although the vehicle was new, little was done to re-vamp the range of colour options available, despite assertions to the contrary in the text of one brochure produced in 1967. In the last year of Splittie production, the line-up to supplement the perennial Dove Blue had been Light Grey, Velvet Green and Pearl White, at least as far as the 'commercial' vehicles went. For the Bay the spectrum was identical save that, at long last, Neptune Blue succeeded Dove (a shade so similar that many wouldn't even have noticed anyway).

As for the Microbuses, the staple Splittie options, namely Lotus White and Titian Red, were carried forward, although the all-new shade of Neptune Blue was joined by another sparkling addition, Savannah Beige. With the exception of the all Lotus White Microbus L, all other shades were complemented by a roof panel painted in Cloud White when the top of the range model was presented. Gone were the days of the genuine two-tone Bus, but soon that would be the least of VW's worries when it came to the more upmarket offerings.

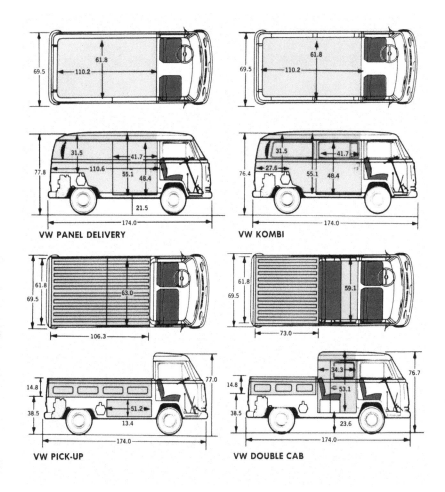

VW PANEL DELIVERY

VW KOMBI

VW PICK-UP

VW DOUBLE CAB

STANDARD EQUIPMENT

- Adjustable driver's seat and backrest
- Ashtray
- Back-up lights
- Bumpers, front and rear
- Coat hooks
- Directional signals (wrap-around in front)
- Dished steering wheel
- Dome lights, cab and cargo area (Panel Delivery and Kombi) Dome light cab area only (Pick-up and Double Cab)
- Dual padded sunvisors
- Electric 2-speed windshield wipers
- Four-way safety flashers
- Fresh-air heater/defroster and ventilation system
- Electric rear window defogger
- Glovebox with door

- Break-away inside rear view mirror
- Outside rear view mirrors, left and right
- Leatherette headliner in cab
- Leatherette upholstery
- Lockable storage compartment (under bed of Pick-ups)
- Non-repeat ignition/steering lock
- Padded instrument panel
- Roll-down windows in cab
- Seat belts for all seats
- Side safety reflectors
- Sliding loading door on side (Kombi and Panel)
- Spare wheel and tire
- Split front seat and aisle (Kombi and Panel)
- Twelve volt battery with early cut-in 540 watts generator
- Windshield washer

COLORS Montana Red, Lotus White and Neptune Blue.

"The most efficient way to carry most things is in a box. So you'd think there wouldn't be much we could do to improve our box-on-wheels, right?"

From its introduction as a useful option on the first-generation Splittie package, a sliding door was always only available at extra cost. Ditto the aisle between the front seats. Somebody in marketing worked out a good Bay sales pitch in this respect. Thanks to both Splittie options becoming standard features with the Bay, the "combination [could] cut a deliveryman's in-and-out-time by 20 or 30 seconds each call, which could add up to 35 or 40 minutes a day."

Although the Bay could carry a little more than its predecessor, due to its marginally increased size (those useful brochure writers even calculating the gain – 165lb more in boxes and parcels, or 6.6ft^3), the real improvements came in other ways.

A US copywriter said it best: "The dashboard is all new. We recessed the dials to make them easier to read. Replaced our open under-dash parcel shelf with a huge glove compartment (with a door). Then padded the entire panel and covered it with black vinyl. We tilted the steering wheel toward the driver, moved the gearshift lever closer and added a pistol-grip to the parking brake. We made the driver's seat slide back and forth to nine positions – and added a rotary knob that adjusts the seatback to an infinite number of angles within a 14 degree arc."

Additionally, the ventilation system was different with demister outlets below the windshield, wind-up-and-down rather than slide-backwards-and-forwards cab side windows, bigger wipers, wider access doors and ingenious rubber-matted bumper ends to make cab access easier.

Metal for the high-jump with the High-Roof Delivery Van

In a break with Splittie tradition, albeit a recently established one, the Bay 'high-roof' was made of fibreglass rather than metal, being almost kit-car like in its conception. While aesthetically repugnant, looking like an over-turned bathtub, the vehicle sold. After all, practicality rather than elegance was king when it came to a Panelvan.

"The VW High-Roofed Delivery Van isn't just ideal for boutique owners ... it's the ideal solution for all outsize, light-weight bulk goods."

Jack of all trades – the Kombi – seating extra!

"The VW Kombi is supplied in different versions from country to country." You bet! In Canada the message was that the Kombi had "two big side windows and a vent on either side. Which may come in handy should you ever wish to carry passengers. Because you can buy it with seats as an optional extra." No wonder it was named the 'VW Window Van' in some markets. Elsewhere the more conventional message was that there were "ten different seating configurations. The VW Kombi can seat up to eight and in comfort."

Volkswagen gets a 'clip' round the ear!

Then for an ill-chosen name and now for loss of identity

Although we might often refer to the icing on the cake of the Splittie range as the Samba, either in its early 23-window guise or its later 21-portal appearance, its official name was always the Microbus Deluxe.

However, with the advent of the Bay, flamboyance briefly reigned supreme, for the new top of the range models were known as the Clipper and Clipper L, accordingly. However, someone hadn't done his or her homework. Airline company, BOAC had been running a Clipper Class of flights to North America for a few years and not unreasonably objected to Volkswagen's high-jacking of its name and a short but acrimonious tangle followed. The car giant beat a hasty retreat and henceforth the name Microbus was re-instated,

although occasionally today someone might still be heard to whisper the Clipper name.

Perhaps then the selected photo, taken from a brochure produced just after VW had conceded ignominious defeat, has a hint of irony in its composition. Glancing again at the image, few can fail to notice that whereas the range-topping Splittie stood out in a crowd, the Clipper L could almost be mistaken for a Kombi, if it wasn't for its contrasting roof panel. Bearing in mind, that some Microbuses came in single colours such as Lotus White, or Savannah Beige, surely the copywriters had some serious marketing to do? Not a bit of it, for the Microbus and Microbus L sold just as well as their respective predecessors.

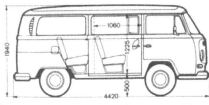

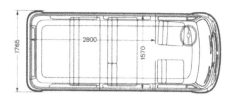

1230 mm = 48.4 in.	1940 mm = 76.4 in.	1060 mm = 41.7 in.
730 mm = 28.7 in.	4420 mm = 174.0 in.	1225 mm = 48.2 in.

2800 mm = 110.2 in.	500 mm = 19.7 in.
1570 mm = 61.8 in.	1765 mm = 69.5 in.

2. Open wide and say ah!

In the States, advertising aces Doyle Dane Bernbach had got the new Bay or VW Station-Wagon sussed. The message was deliciously simple. Trouble was, the imagery, or at least the reproduction in the 1969 brochure depicted here, left more than a little to be desired. Like the brochure's title? *The Car that comes in a box*. Thought you would!

"The big difference between a Volkswagen Station Wagon and other station wagons is the box ours comes in. Other wagons are basically sedans. With extra carrying space tagged onto the back end. Ours is basically a big carrying space ... once you understand these basics, you begin to see the Volkswagen Station Wagon for what it really is. Not the wagon that looks best. But the one that gets full last. That's the beauty of it."

Each page told the same story, simply and effectively. "A car you can feel at home in." Plenty of space. "A car with guest room." More space than the neighbours. "A car with room to handle things no other car can handle." 170ft² of space. "A car you can handle where there's not enough room for other cars." A vehicle, for all its space, that was no bigger than those with lots less space. Now you appreciate the page title – open wide and say wow!

3. A Volkswagen history lesson

The death of Heinz Nordhoff in April 1968 could easily have spelled the premature demise of the Bay, despite its buoyant sales performance. First of the air-cooled models to go under the new regime was the razor edge Karmann Ghia, the coach-built 'sports' car based on the VW 1500/1600, its demise having been predicted and then confirmed in July 1969. Next, in July 1973, was the VW 1600, a car that at the time of Nordhoff's death was being produced at the rate of a quarter of a million vehicles per annum. The much loved Beetle-based Karmann Ghia's lengthy production run came to an end in July 1974, while the ill-fated 411/412, conceived in Nordhoff's final years but launched a few months after his death, was dropped at the same time.

Kurt Lotz, Nordhoff's immediate successor, had been determined to rid Volkswagen of its star performer, the Beetle, and while he had fallen from grace by the autumn of 1971, he had sufficiently turned the tables against the old regime that his successor, Rudolph Leiding, had little option but to plough ahead with plans for a very different fleet of Volkswagens. The water-cooled, front-wheel drive, Passat was the first of the new generation to go into production, which it did in May 1973. In January 1974 it was followed by the Golf, in February of the same year by the sporty Scirocco and in March 1975 by the Polo. As for the Beetle, having first been exiled to the Emden plant, production finally ceased in Germany, if not in the South American satellites, at the beginning of January 1978.

Now, doesn't that explain a lot?

Throughout this period of turmoil the Bay more than just plodded along. Lotz seemed to regard it with far less enmity than any of the other air-cooled models. Leiding had other issues on his mind and it was only when he resigned at the beginning of 1975 that the next Director General, Toni Schmücker, set in motion plans for its successor, to be realised when the design had been on the road for a lengthy 12 years.

Nordhoff left behind him a profitable organisation, realising 339 million DM for the bank account in the year of his death. When Volkswagen was liberated from Lotz's clutches that figure had shrunk to a miserly 12 million DM, as money was squandered on the back of one bad decision after another. Leiding initially seemed to stem the flow, but the vast investments required to develop the new generation meant that by 1974 an unprecedented loss of 555 million DM was recorded.

It is against this background that the Bay survived and prospered. While little in the way of cash was spent on it, merely giving it a reasonably cheap-to-implement facelift once and a series of 'off-the-shelf' engines when customers complained about its lack of oomph, the Bay toughed it out and in the darkest years of all turned in some remarkable production figures.

4. Power surge lights up the Bay?

Twin-sets and little perforations

Compare the typically bland frontal shot of a Bay depicted left. It could be a '68 year model or a '69, '70, '71, or even a '72. In reality it's a 1970 model and comes courtesy of Volkswagen Canada. Now check out the wheels on the Bay below. That's right, its got flat hubcaps, surrounded by circular holes on the inner wheel rim. Those are the only visible clues to date it to the '71 model year improvements.

For the '70 model year, Volkswagen's copywriters placed an emphasis on 'more safety', this having arrived in the shape of additional body rigidity, strengthened inner doorframes and a collapsible steering column. For the '71 model they stressed that the engine had been revamped, with mention of disc brakes being thrown in for good measure. Modified cylinder heads had two inlet ports nestled side-by-side, instead of the previous single arrangement. Not only did the engine run more smoothly

and breathe with greater efficiency, but also the power output increased to 50bhp at a maximum of 4000rpm. To owners of the new engine, who had previously experienced the single port version, here was a great improvement. Whether Volkswagen thought the increased power of the engine demanded improved stopping power, or the fitting of discs up front was coincidental, remains anyone's guess. Until the '71 model year, the wheels on the Bay had been of exactly the same size and design as those fitted to later Splitties. With the arrival of discs, increased ventilation was demanded resulting in the old design of four narrow cooling slots being replaced by the series of round holes (already referred to) being punched through the inner rim. To complete the picture, the new wheels were a little broader, allowing fitment of slightly beefier tyres (previously 5J x 14in – now 5½J x 14in).

Extra oomph for the open road

With disc brakes up-front and radial tyres fitted, when the Seventeen powered it, the Bay was ready to meet all-comers.

While the 1600 engine would soldier on to the end of Bay production in 1979, in August 1971, for the '72 model year, a 1.7-litre engine filched from the VW 411 joined old faithful. Confusingly, all American Bays benefited from the extra power afforded by the 1679cc unit, whereas in Europe the Pick-up was excluded from the fun. Complex in its engineering, the Seventeen nevertheless produced an argument-quashing 66bhp at 4800rpm. Bore and stroke stood at 90 x 66mm respectively, while twin Solex 34 PDSIT carbs helped the Bay to flow at a top speed of 76mph, while the 0-60mph sprint was covered in an almost respectable 22 seconds. Lifting the engine lid was something of a surprise as the Seventeen bore little resemblance to its smaller brother. The cooling fan had been enlarged and mounted on the end of the crankshaft at the rear of the engine, while the aluminium fan housing not only bolted over the fan but also over the top of engine.

Altogether flatter, the new, or rather 'borrowed', engine had already been given the nickname 'suitcase' (yet another piece of unofficial Volkswagen terminology to digest). To improve access to the new power plant, the Bay's engine lid was increased in size, while the previously detachable valance below the lid was now welded into place; a pestiferous move if ever there was one.

Got the engine now, so see how it performs!

"VW has put all the increased power of the new ...1700 into improving lugging power ... This big bodied vehicle is streets ahead of the earlier 1500/1600 models in performance ... In addition, gradient ability is substantially improved: the new model will take a 1 in 16 gradient in top, compared to the old model's best of 1 in 22." *Car*, South Africa.

"A welcome surprise was the lively performance which comes from the 1679cm^3 four-cylinder, air-cooled engine ... It gives the Microbus surging acceleration ... and enables it to cruise at around its maximum speed of 122km/h (76mph) indefinitely ...' *Technicar*.

The Bay: comparing the

To appreciate the full impact of the bodywork changes inflicted/bestowed on the Bay in August 1972, flick between this page and the image of the vehicle as launched at the start of the chapter. Do you know which you like best? Thought so!

The marketing men were proud of the new-look Bay: "This year we've strengthened the bumpers, raised the indicators, so that people can see where they are going. And put the cab steps inside the doors. That VW symbol on the front isn't just for looks. It means something. Craftsmanship, reliability, economy and quality."

Hmm! That the bumpers were improved in terms of absorbing energy was true,

class of '73 with that of '68

but the chunky, almost girder-like, look could easily appear heavy, overweight or even obese! Further, the loss of the Bay's external cab entry step might have been in line with contemporary trends but resulted in a vehicle that oozed less character and exhibited fewer aspects of Volkswagen's traditional, even conservative, approach to vehicle design. Repositioning the indicators was a decidedly odd move; the argument that they were more visible simply didn't hold water. Even the out of favour Beetle would soon have its indicators repositioned lower on the body – as close to the ground as the bumper even (except in the US market)!

Safety first

"That VW symbol on the front isn't just for looks," the copywriter declared. True! Behind the scenes work had improved the Bay's specification without question. Mention has already been made of the strengthened inner frames in 1970. With these had come stiffened body hoops – the members rising from the floor to reinforce the main roof panel – resulting in a more rigid body. For the '72 model year, the louvred air intakes had been increased in size and made squarer to 'suit' the new 1700 engine. Glance above to view the chunkier and more prominent taillights first fitted at the same time. Now, alongside the chunkier bumpers et al, the cab floor had been tweaked to include a crumple zone, a commendable safety feature in the event of a head-on collision. Nevertheless, the symbolic message behind the reduction in size of the VW roundel and its repositioning lower down on the Bay's front panel – the final noteworthy amendment to the vehicle's looks for the '73 model year – was one of playing down a legacy of the Nordhoff era. Let the Bay make money for Volkswagen, the company certainly needed it, but other water-cooled issues were of paramount importance.

Automatically slower?

Primarily with the American market in mind, Volkswagen offered the 1700 engine with an automatic box as an extra-cost option on the '73 model. A three-speed affair, much more in keeping with the times than the semi-auto offered on the Beetle back in 1968, the Bay's torque converter proved to be more reliable and smoother in operation than the offerings of most rival manufacturers. Perhaps surprisingly, performance was relatively unaffected.

VW of America spec sheet 1973: SAE net hp 63/4800rpm, automatic 59/4200rpm. Performance top speed 78mph, with automatic 75mph.

The VW Wagon.

It's more than one auto-journalist bargained for.

Verdict on the VW: "Capable and delightful to drive."

"The 1973 models incorporate substantial styling, detail and mechanical improvements ... To start with, the amber front indicators are bigger and mounted higher ... the bumpers, front and rear, are deeper and heavier this year, to match standard car-bumper heights and give increased protection ... The steering wheel remains very large – the only truck-like feature in the controls of the Microbus – but the steering itself has been made 20 per cent lighter by increasing the ratio of the worm-and-roller system ... The three-speed automatic transmission is the VW unit as used on the Type 4 models ... the best figures were achieved by simply flooring the pedal and letting the gearbox computer do the work ... because of its swift and accurate upshifts and easy use of full power, the Microbus Automatic proved surprisingly nippy in starts from robots [traffic lights] and up to normal expressway speeds. It never held the traffic up and could eat up expressways with the best of them. Its weakness is in hill climbing ... The 1700 engine of the Microbus Automatic is a slightly down-rated version in terms of power, but strong on torque ... It proved very good on economy as well, returning almost exactly the same figures as the manual-shift model ... Anyone who is prepared to pay the very nominal extra cost of the automatic transmission, is sure to be delighted with its service." Road test, *Car*, South Africa, May 1973.

"The new model is about 30 per cent faster in the standard 0-100kph sprint." *Car*

Transitory, that was the 1700 engine, for in August 1973 out popped what would prove to be another equally short-lived incarnation of the flat-four. With oil crises looming large to further aggravate Volkswagen's precarious financial position, it's not surprising that the new engine was shared with, or downloaded from, the VW 412. Built to exactly the same design as the 1700, the increase in capacity was possible thanks to widened cylinder bores (from 90mm to 93mm). Power output rose to 68bhp, which at face value seemed hardly worthwhile considering the 1700 pumped out 66bhp. Maximum speed was likewise barely different, with Volkswagen suggesting an increase of just 4mph. However, the really useful improvement was in the realms of torque, which rose from 81lb/ft at 3200rpm to 92.4lb/ft at 3000rpm. Owners pushing their Bays up hills were only too aware of the difference! As the 1800 had to work less hard for a living than its predecessor, the amount of fuel consumed on a run decreased. As usual, Volkswagen officially proffered conservative consumption figures (22mpg according to Volkswagen UK, 1974 models brochure) but most drivers, even those encumbered with a heavy right foot, could expect to achieve in the region of 26mpg.

While twin carbs were still a feature of the engines of European Bays fitted with the larger power unit, across in the United States Bosch fuel injection became the order of the day in most states.

2-litre family transportation doesn't have to be dull

August 1975 played host to the debut of the final, and beefiest, of all air-cooled engines, a 1970cc, or 2-litre offering, boasting a full 70bhp. Before rejoicing over an engine designed specifically for the Bay, the VW 412 by this time being dead and truly buried, think of the VW-Porsche 914 – the mid-engined joint project sports vehicle, which had made its debut at the Frankfurt motor show in 1969. Yes, the 2-litre engine had been introduced to that car in 1973 and now it was conveniently wedged into the Bay. The bore and stroke were 94mm and 71mm respectively, with maximum power being achieved at 4200rpm. Twin carbs were fitted for most markets but, inevitably, customers in the USA were endowed with the Bosch fuel injection. Top speed was now a lusty 80mph according to Volkswagen, but many owners could just about make the ton, that is once the 2-litre had a few thousand miles under its belt. A further eight per cent increase in torque assisted with hill climbing once more.

Sadly, the marketing men didn't go out of their way to promote the 2-litre engine or, for that matter, many aspects of Bays produced in the latter years. One respected author on the subject even went so far as to claim that, by 1976, "Volkswagen admitted that development of the second-generation Transporter was over" – an opinion no doubt voiced after reading what the copywriters had to say. In 1979, a few months away from the debut of the Wedge, the engines available were dismissed in a single short paragraph. "Choose from the frugal standard 1.6-litre (50bhp) or the powerful 2-litre (70bhp) engines and you have all the advantages of air-cooled engines. They won't boil or freeze and have no water hoses, radiator or water pump to let you down. The larger engine has brake servo and radial ply tyres as standard and is also available with manual or automatic transmission." With all other models in Volkswagen's range by this time pumping water vigorously, retention of the old clichés in the text seemed odd. Clearly the copywriter knew what lay ahead. However, as far as shouting from the rooftops about the Bay's merits went, well that was now clearly a job for the auto-press.

5. Round up – Bay boasts

Full flow on the Bay

"On the road the 2-litre ... is equally impressive. The twin-carb Type 4 engine delivers 70bhp, offering performance which makes it much more enjoyable to drive than the 1600cc version. It will out accelerate many cars and easily cruise at the legal limit on motorways, regardless of headwinds or hills. The 0-60mph time is 21 seconds, top speed is about 80mph and the 30-50mph acceleration in top gear takes only 13.2 seconds ... Overtaking presents no problems and I found it just as easy to drive as a car and capable of averaging practically the same speeds on a typical journey ... According to the government figures, the 2-litre engine is also more economical at a steady speed [than the 1600]. My overall average fuel consumption was 22mpg including a lot of 70mph motorway travelling with five adults and two children on board." *Safer VW Motoring*, May 1979

"The test car ... proved to be the fastest of the 2-litre Kombi models we have tested, topping 130[kph] on a level road and sprinting to 90 in 16.7 seconds. With a big-bodied vehicle the gearshift has to be used more than with a five-seat car, but the Microbus is pleasing to drive. It also achieves

fair economy in relation to seating and load capacity, logging 11.5 litres/100km (24.6mpg) at 90 for a 480km cruising range potential. It braked exceptionally well for its size." *Car South Africa*, March 1979

"To sum up, the automatic-transmissioned VW van, at some $6100, taxes, freight and license included price, may be a bit more expensive than some domestic products. What it offers is either passenger or cargo capability, reasonable economy, great all-round visibility, definitely improved horsepower and performance, an acceptable degree of off-road performance, a very comfortable ride and precise handling ... in 27 years of development and refinement Volkswagen has had the last laugh." *PV4*, January 1977

"The flat-4 used in the '76 model Bus was lifted directly from the late lamented Porsche 914. With two litres of displacement, even our automatic version could easily keep up with traffic and even out-accelerate a car or two. We loved it. The feeling of driving a VW Bus that was fast was marvellous ... One of the nicest features of the Bus is that its gas mileage doesn't change much with load ... The VW Bus is still the best buy in a van type of vehicle for passenger use. Recent currency fluctuations have caused its price to rise a lot, but you can't get the same thing anywhere else for less and you certainly can't run anything else for less." *Complete Volkswagen Book*, 1976

compared to the Splittie model breakdown, the Panelvan Bay lost its pole position to both the Microbus and the Kombi, at least until the mid-seventies. Could it be that the enormous growth of the camper van in the Bay area, multitudinous offerings of which were less frequently glued into the Panelvan, was a determining factor?

The best Bay year of all was 1972, when 259,101 examples rolled off the assembly line. From that point, although

"It's more fun when your crowd can spread out – and stay together."

That the Bay was an enormous success can never be denied. Between its launch in August 1967 and the day it bowed out at the end of July 1979, 2,465,000 Bays had been built at the Hanover and Emden factories alone.

Satellite operations in Brazil, South Africa, Australia and Mexico accounted for more – a good number more. In its 17-year run the Splittie notched up a commendable figure totalling a little under 2 million sales. The Bay did more than this, half a million more to be precise, in just 12 years. Its successor, the Wedge, just couldn't stand the pace by comparison.

Curiously, however, when

IT'S MORE FUN WHEN YOUR CROWD CAN SPREAD OUT

the figures remained respectable – never falling below the 150,000 mark – sales gradually tailed away. Was it simply that other manufacturers had caught up? After all there had been 22 years for them to get their respective acts together. Or was it that the relatively recently introduced Japanese imports were on the warpath? Had the oil crises of the mid-1970s been decisive? No, the simple answer was that in the new water-cooled world of Volkswagen, the old Nordhoff

philosophy of continual improvement – something that encompassed much more than simply forcing a new engine into the Bay – had been more or less forgotten. Although by the time the 2-litre engine made its debut, the top of the range Microbus L had acquired alloy waistline strips lined up with the Bay's door handles, a retracting step to help the less able to hop-up through the sliding side door and the option of a heated rear window, while Kombi owners and above could splash-out on tinted window glass, these were in reality trivialities. Halogen bulbs, radial tyres and thicker front discs were improvements, but little was said.

Let's end the story of the Bay with a typically bland bit of marketing speak extracted from a 1979 brochure intended for the British market. Comprehensive it might be, inspiring it certainly isn't.

"Microbus L: Based on the Microbus, the luxurious Microbus L comes complete with a host of additional interior and exterior

equipment such as two-tone paint, chrome bumpers with rubber inserts, radial tyres, reversing lights, electric clock, vanity mirror, extra trim and wall-to-wall carpeting in the luggage compartment. Whether you choose the Microbus L as a prestigious personnel carrier or a deluxe estate car you'll be surrounded by luxury."

STAY TOGETHER.

1. 'Airing' on the side of conservatism

A shock was in store for would-be purchasers of Volkswagen's third generation Transporter, the Type 25. While it might have been modern in appearance and visually a worthy successor to the Bay, its outer shell masked a quirky conservatism.

May 1979 heralded the start of production of Volkswagen's latest Transporter in preparation for its launch in August. Without any doubt the latest model was a marketing man's nightmare, as its very makeup flew in the face of everything the re-born Volkswagen was already successfully promoting. Its looks, though very different from its two predecessors, were fine, and (with the exception of a humped bonnet up-front housing the engine) certainly very 'eighties', even if this bigger and rather slab-shaped Bus received the unflattering nickname of 'Wedge'. The problem for copywriters was the engine. Wasn't the Beetle dead, if not completely buried? Weren't the Golf and its siblings all-conquering, at least at Castle Wolfsburg? Yet here in the Wedge was a spectre of times past: an air-cooled, rear-mounted, flat-four engine, most definitely of the old school.

Truth to tell, it's difficult to explain why the newly appointed VW boss, Toni Schmücker, had decreed in May 1975 that the Wedge would be air-cooled. Admittedly, the water-cooled cars hadn't really proven themselves at this point, but there was more than a hint that all would be well. Perhaps there was a reluctance to commit yet more development money at a time when the firm was up to its ears in accumulated debts caused by the creation of the water-pumper fleet. Surely there can be little doubt that it was more than a simple lack of experience on the part of the ex-Ford man. Who knows?

Possibly complacency was the reason. Records confirm that Schmücker believed competition from other manufacturers to the concept of a box-on-wheels was still non-existent, thanks to its "particular design and mechanics". With such assertions the new Director General was sadly mistaken. The design department, under Gustav Meyer, groaned in disappointment, the marketing men wrung their hands in anguish; both had been keen to break the commercial mould. The future looked bleak to them, but, amazingly, the time was only just around the corner when they would get their way after all.

Disclaimer (this and previous page): the Wedge was available from day one as a complete range (just like the Bay had been before it). Sadly, as with the rest of VW's promotional literature at the time, illustrative material produced in Europe to promote the Wedge was less than inspirational. The best of a bad bunch has been eked out of a multiplicity of nondescript brochures. Typical, then, that it was as late as 1983 before a shot could be located of the range – this dates from later than that too. Try to blot out of your minds the second and smaller grille located between the turn indicators. Thanks too to Volkswagen of America for the majority of the more inspirational shots over the next 20-plus pages.

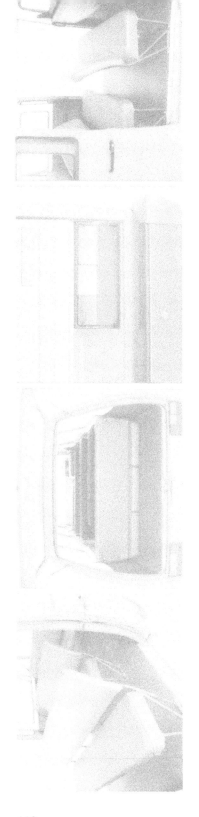

Wedge branding – and Brick attributes

Gone (allegedly) were the days when the Transporter was simply that. From now on such a derogatory name applied purely to the lower-orders, or 'goods vehicles' in the range, while the posh people carriers were bestowed the American sounding title of 'Bus', at least for a year or two. Of course, there was a technical hitch to all this, in that Volkswagen of America had already adopted the name 'Vanagon' for its latest 'commercial' offering, no doubt to complement the equally suspect term of 'Campmobile', which had been on the go in US Volkswagen circles for a good number of years.

Although at first glance the Wedge possessed as much aesthetic charm as a contemporary high-rise block of flats, gaining in the process a second, even more unflattering, nickname of the 'brick', nevertheless in some respects it represented another step forward in commercial vehicle production.

The solemn, almost menacing-faced, Wedge, at least when compared to the smiley Splittie and the welcoming Bay, benefited from a better drag co-efficiency and had blossomed in all the right places.

The designers had utilised the space available far better than they had with the new model's predecessors.

Let the copywriters take up the story: "As far as alterations to dimensions are concerned, the width has been increased by almost 125mm (5in) and the length by 65mm (2½in). Yet parking is still no problem. The slightly longer wheelbase and wider track give a turning circle of 10.7m (35ft). Height has not been affected. Thus access to garages and multi story car parks is as good as ever it was."

Most impressive was the enlargement in width. To give some sort of practical demonstration, three-people could sit in the front with much greater comfort than in the Splittie or Bay, a factor that was unquestionably an important selling point in a number of markets. The 65mm increase in length by contrast seemed small-fry, although it did allow one US copywriter to come up with a mind boggling if obscure comparison – "[With] an outside only a foot longer than a Porsche."

Strictly speaking, the sales people were wrong to state that there had been no boost in height: that is if 10mm counts for anything. However, thanks to the Wedge's flat roof, the increase seemed far greater.

"Space is what counts, making the most of it inside," revealed the text of a US brochure dating from 1982

Thanks to a controversial lowering of the rear-loading platform (to be discussed shortly) to 825mm (32.5in) and a less controversial new design to 455mm (17.9in) at the side, the Wedge could carry bulkier items. As the draftsman's pen succumbed to the might of the machine, the computer-designed floor-pan allowed a 100mm less exerting step up into the vehicle, while doing away with the old cross members. The result was a lower centre of gravity and a decrease in weight, which meant that heavier parcels could be bundled into the Panelvan, as permissible loading weights increased to close on one metric tonne. Even the spare wheel found a new home: this time located out of harm's way in a hinged metal tray, upfront but underneath the body, forward of the front wheels.

Increases in track size made the Wedge more stable. At the front the leap was from 1395mm to 1570mm, at the rear a slightly gentler addition prevailed, up from 1455mm to 1570mm. Long

gone were the days of skinny cross-ply tyres, with beefy 185-80 x 14 radials standard to all variants where the larger of the two engines was fitted. However, the worker bee vans with base model specifications remained on 7.00 x 14 8PR cross-ply tyres. On the suspension front, sadly Volkswagen's hallmark torsion bars were both costly to manufacture and bulky in the space they occupied. As a result, the new front suspension was by double wishbones, progressive coil springs, with inner telescopic shock absorbers and an anti-roll bar. At the back, suspension was by trailing arms, telescopic dampers and coil springs, which was certainly less radical in its changes.

Bearing more than a passing visual resemblance to Volkswagen's larger commercial vehicles, the water-cooled LT range (which had been launched as recently as April 1975), the stylists went some way in considering the Wedge's aerodynamics in order to squeeze an extra dribble or two of fuel out between wallet emptying calls at the filling station. In the process they also encouraged higher top speeds out of the two essentially old, if not entirely anachronistic, engines offered at launch.

"Bigger, bolder and more beautiful than ever" (*Car*, South Africa)

At the front, the Wedge's structure assumed more of a curve, while the area above the air-intake grille was raked at the steepest of angles. A larger, similarly curved windscreen dominated the vehicle's stance, amounting in total to a generous 21 per cent more glass than that of the Bay. Round headlamps, albeit now incorporated into a modern looking (though entirely fake) radiator grille, plus the retention of a (sadly shrunken) VW roundel, helped to demonstrate that here was a product still in the traditional VW mould.

At the rear, vision had been increased by a truly extravagant 92 per cent, while in a perverse sort of way the Splittie's barn door had re-emerged. The tailgate, which ran from the top of the vehicle to a position well below its waistline, was top-hinged and supported by dampers on either side. As a distinct negative there was no separate engine lid, which meant that, in true VW 1500/1600 and VW 411/412 style, access was via a removable panel in the rear luggage compartment. An ingenious flip-down arrangement involving the license plate revealed the oil-filler cap, at least ensuring that the Type 25's lifeblood wasn't entirely ignored.

Unquestionably slab-like when viewed from the side, the Wedge's appearance was really only broken or softened by

a waist-level swage line and a complementary, if less distinct, one that ran around the vehicle's lower body. The situation was accentuated by that virtually flat roof already referred to, which, while allowing more headroom for passengers, lacked the rounded and more homely feeling of the Bay. Even the engine ventilation slots, unceremoniously stacked behind the rear passenger windows when these arose, appeared meaner and less rounded. The cab doors were considerably wider, affording both easier access and, unfortunately, ample opportunity to scrape the paintwork when parked in tight spaces. The Wedge's sliding door assumed patio-style proportions, making both loading and passenger access even easier than it had been with the Bay.

Whereas the first water-cooled models from the Volkswagen stable, just like the Bay, featured little in the way of safeguards against corrosion, the Wedge was generously daubed with a rubberised protection on all its seams, while the injection of wax into the body cavities helped Volkswagen to claim a degree of longevity for its product. Sadly, as Wedges age not entirely gracefully, that very defence of the seams causes problems as it becomes brittle with time, and the ingress of both water and salt is inevitably followed by tin-worm.

SAFETY FIRST, TRIMMINGS NEXT AND 'SHADES' LAST

Sometimes it's hard to better the text of a half-competent copywriter and when it comes to the advances in safety offered by the Wedge, even at the expense of being a tad repetitious, it's worth quoting just about the lot. Perhaps, too, it's worth a note to say that if the writer was clever enough, he could disguise design features as old as the hills as attractive innovations.

"One of the safety features is the sophisticated chassis. This incorporates the double wishbones and an anti-roll bar in front, semi-trailing arm rear axle. Independent suspension all round. Another feature is the dual-circuit brake system with a brake pressure regulator and, now on all vehicles, a brake servo. An important safety aspect is obviously the road holding. This is achieved by the drive concept, which puts the weight of the driver in front, the weight of the engine at the back and the load in the middle." (Can this really be the same marketing team that was charged with the task of selling the Golf and its brethren?) "The fuel tank and the spare wheel have now been relocated to the front of the vehicle to balance the axle loadings. Naturally enough, the Volkswagen Commercials were subjected to extensive crash testing.

This enabled a well thought out safety system to be built in. First, the impact of a collision is absorbed by the front bumper and transmitted to a deformation element running the full width of it. This element, in turn, is mounted on a forked frame with pre-programmed deformation points in the floor assembly. Other safety features include the safety steering column with a detachable coupling and two flexible struts, collapsible struts under the dashboard and door reinforcements."

Wrap-round front indicators, situated lower on the body than they had been on later Bays, painted black safety

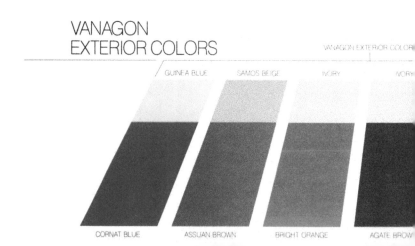

VANAGON
EXTERIOR COLORS

VANAGON EXTERIOR COLOR

GUINEA BLUE   SAMOS BEIGE   IVORY   IVORY

CORNAT BLUE   ASSUAN BROWN   BRIGHT ORANGE   AGATE BROWN

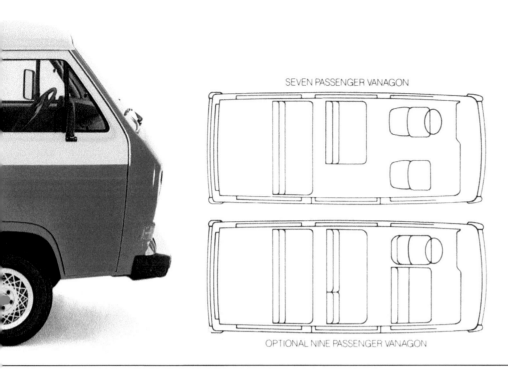

SEVEN PASSENGER VANAGON

OPTIONAL NINE PASSENGER VANAGON

handles and larger exterior rear view mirrors were other definite plus points, while Volkswagen's copywriters claimed yet another in the shape of the Wedge's bumpers. Few nowadays would regard the cheap girder-style bumpers, with their nasty black plastic end caps as even vaguely desirable, even if they did allegedly offer more protection than those hung on the Bay and, earlier, the Splittie.

The Microbus L, or Bus L to be precise, more or less defied the plain-Jane plastic look demanded by the latest trend gurus not just at Volkswagen but also right across

the vehicle-manufacturing world. For not only did it boast half-respectable chrome bumpers (equipped with rubber inserts and regrettably those black plastic end pieces), it also bragged alloy trim mouldings which were set into all the window rubbers, tapped onto the otherwise denuded slab sides, encased the fresh air intake grille on the front panel and entwined the rain gutters on the outside of the windscreen pillars. Whether the Bus L looked liked a twinkly, sparkly, modern Romany caravan has to be a subjective decision. The paint combinations too, once highly fashionable,

might now languish in the doldrums of bad-taste, but will no doubt re-emerge refreshed after a suitable lapse of time.

While Ivory over Brilliant Orange might simply be classed as loud, and Guinea Blue over Cornat Blue as startling, Ivory over Agate Brown and Samos Beige over Assuan Brown have to be candidates for an immediate respray. Thank goodness the worker bee Buses were not subjected to such treatment, and the traditional Dove and Neptune Blue of previous generations was replaced by a straightforward Medium Blue on the Wedge.

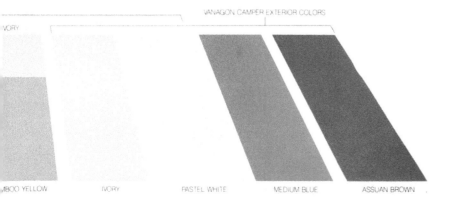

VANAGON CAMPER EXTERIOR COLORS

IVORY

IBOO YELLOW   IVORY   PASTEL WHITE   MEDIUM BLUE   ASSUAN BROWN

"THE NEW BUS. SUCH A LOT TO OFFER."

A.

B.

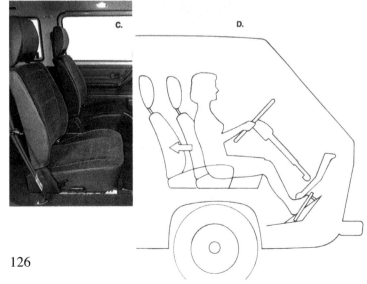

C.

D.

Diving into the Wedge's interior, it wouldn't have taken even a casual observer long to see that the stylists had given the vehicle a full and bang up-to-date makeover. While it was both easy and satisfying to imagine that you were sat behind the wheel of a Passat or Golf of similar vintage, there was an inevitable consequence: gone forever were the timeless qualities of both the Bay and particularly post-'55 Splitties.

The third generation Transporter's dashboard was made almost entirely out of plastic, but whether this was to save weight or money, depends on how cynical your viewpoint is. The binnacle shrouded a veritable feast of gauges and rocker type switches compared to previous years, with superfluous items like clocks becoming the norm, even though a blanking panel for the extra-cost option radio had pride of place in the centre of the dashboard. The glove box was large, while the steering wheel, though lacking panache, looked far less like one borrowed from an artic.

Most thought that the seats were improved, with a greater degree of lateral support and, where vinyl was the option rather than cloth, the material design was relatively smooth making cleaning easier. Although the off-white headlining was a full-length affair for most models, only the top of the range Microbus benefited from covered window pillars, the rest had to make do with painted metal, as in days gone by. When it came to floor coverings, all models except the Microbus were decked out with hardwearing rubber. The passengers in a posh model luxuriated in equally serviceable carpeting. Heating came via exchangers in the traditional air-cooled way and, while it was the subject of criticism, the system remained highly effective, providing genuine VW replacement parts were fitted in later years. Ventilation was improved, with large openings on either side of the dashboard and 'boosters' in the rear passenger compartment.

Vanagon

VANAGON L

NEW JERSEY
385·NZF
·GARDEN STATE·

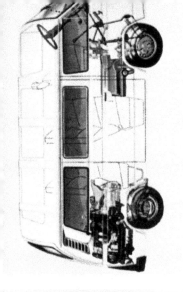

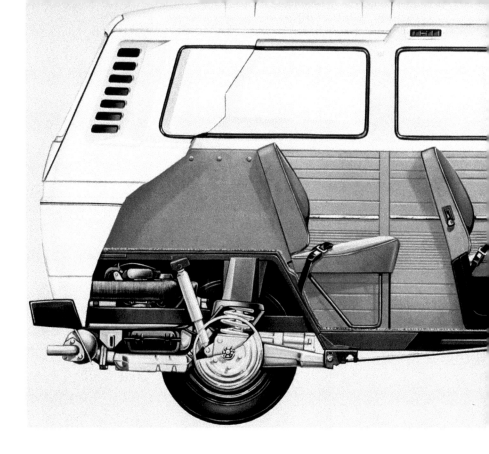

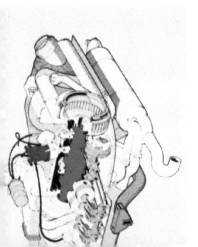

"This drive concept (engine behind the rear axle, driving the rear wheels) has been retained. So too, has Volkswagen's air-cooled engine, renowned for its reliability and durability."

Fully aware of the changing times at Volkswagen, even the most ardent diehards of the old air-cooled days must have been shocked when the Wedge appeared with two variations on the faithful flat-four theme, both of which lacked even the merest hint of a drip of water. One of the two might have made sense, particularly if somewhere along the line there was another vehicle bearing the VW badge, possibly even by default, as was the case with the relatively recently redundant VW Porsche 914, but the 2-litre air-cooled unit had to stand or fall on its own.

Developing 70bhp at 4200rpm, the 2-litre, 1970cc engine, had a bore of 94mm, a stroke of 71mm and a compression ratio of 7.4:1. In Europe, the 2-litre model sported twin 34 PDSIT carburettors, while, in the USA, a Bosch K-Jectronic fuel injection was the norm. In California, a catalytic converter was compulsory which, together with universal measures to restrict emissions of noxious fumes, had the effect of snatching much-needed power from the engine. Check out a US brochure of the day and the SAE listing says it all. The poor Vanagon 2-litre could muster no more than 67bhp (SAE). 0-60mph was achievable in 21.2 seconds according to the US publication *Pick-up, Van and 4WD*. *Road and Track* confirmed this figure when it did its own test stating that this was "not acceleration that will elicit gasps of glee, but it does permit the Vanagon to keep up with everyday, around town traffic". Perhaps the sometimes claimed top cruising speed of 86mph was the required sop to any shortcomings associated with an evermore legislative world, despite VW's own more conservative 78mph for the Delivery

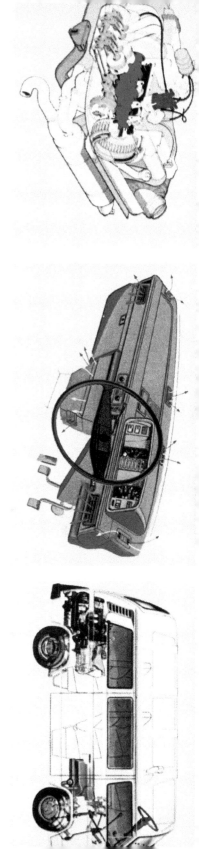

Van and Bus, plus an even slower 76mph for both variations of Pick-up. Conversely, at a time when fuel prices were creeping ever upwards, the 2-litre engine could hardly be described as a portrait of economy. Smooth it might have been, frugal it wasn't. Although figures as low as a wallet-leeching 16.8mpg were bandied about, and acknowledged by VW as such on the urban cycle, at a constant 56mph as much as 25mpg was apparently available.

The 2-litre block was initially the only engine to be offered in the USA, but in Europe the once mighty, and by now incredibly feeble, 1600 was still around, albeit in a modified form. Remember that the luggage compartment at the rear of the vehicle had been increased thanks to a chunk having been taken out of the traditional size of the engine compartment, while full access was now via the cumbersome removal of a carpeted cover and no doubt the goods and chattels of a busy camping weekend, or a day at the shops. Inevitably, the old 1600 engine had to be squashed down, suitcase style. Thanks to the increased weight of the Wedge over a similar Bay, what had been a slow, and hence hardly relaxing drive with the latter turned into a nightmare of continual gear-changes in a desperate attempt to keep up with the fitter cyclist. 50bhp and that was your lot. Maximum speed rolled in at something in the high sixties.

Hydraulic tappets became a feature of both engine options for the first time and, although some today complain that they can take up to 10 minutes to run quietly, at least they did away with the tedious job of frequent manual adjustment. Electronic ignition ensured that the engine stayed in tune longer, while 'Digital Idling Stabilisation', or a computer system without the jargon thrown in, solved the problem of an engine cutting out on a cold morning, or refusing to re-start when hot and bothered.

"THE VANAGON IS A VERY SPECIAL VEHICLE DESIGNED TO MEET A WIDE RANGE OF USAGE WITH REMARKABLE APLOMB." US copywriter

Vanagon

Although many motoring journalists expressed surprise at Volkswagen's choice of engine and its location, few showed serious concern, while the general response to the new Wedge-shaped Transporter must have been music to the ears of Volkswagen's top brass.

Car and Driver was impressed that what it found "draped over the revised chassis" was "one of the handsomer bodies ever tailored for a van". Proceeding to marvel at the "15 per cent increase in the Vanagon's interior volume" and the "40 per cent improvement in rear luggage space", the writer claimed the Wedge to be "the Porsche 911 of vans. The Vanagon goes down the road with a car-like assuredness that's never existed in vehicles of this type before."

Road and Track remarked on the "rich brown carpeting and corduroy seats" of the Vanagon, while noting that the once noisy air-cooled engine was "so well insulated now that it's very subdued inside". *Motor Trend* named the Wedge as its van of the year, sang the praises of the Vanagon as "one of the best utilitarian vehicles ever to take to the highway. Its efficient use of space, attention to ride comfort and sedan-like handling, position it as the new high mark the industry must strive to equal."

Robin Wager, the second editor of Britain's oldest magazine dedicated to Volkswagens, originally *Safer VW Motoring*, now *VW Motoring*, wrote in 1980 of a "splendid carry all". The "2-litre version ... has more or less the old engine, made a little more compact for a lower floor; but everything else about it is new, from the all-round coil spring suspension to the Golf/Polo derived instrument panel ... The old characteristics are still in the engine, which will rev happily (I saw 70mph in third) and helped me to take advantage of the van's new found cornering power."

Nothing else is a Volkswagen

"A VEHICLE THAT USES SO LITTLE FUEL PER PASSENGER MILE NOW GETS AN EVEN THRIFTIER ALTERNATIVE. A DIESEL."

2. Diesel delivery

Buffeted by a worldwide decline in vehicle sales and increased competition, particularly from the Japanese market, almost as soon as the Wedge was launched, Volkswagen had no option but to look at adding more options to the range. The general advances in diesel engine technology meant that Volkswagen, like many other manufacturers, was now offering diesel options for its family cars like the Golf. The logical next step was to use this power unit in the Wedge.

To squeeze the 1588cc diesel engine borrowed from the Golf into the Transporter, the in-line four was tilted at a 50° angle. Developing 54bhp in the Golf, the same unit offered 50bhp as maximum power was delivered at 4200rpm instead of 4800. Maximum torque however was boosted to 76lb/ft at just 2000rpm. Other differences related to a larger flywheel, plus both a heavy-duty clutch and oil cooler to regulate temperatures that you would expect of a vehicle designed to carry heavier loads.

With more effort required to kick a diesel into life than with the petrol engine versions, the starter motor output was increased to 1.7kw, while a 63ah battery was installed, rather than the standard 45ah affair.

Bearing in mind the sluggish nature of the 1600 petrol engine Wedge, perhaps some would have been looking for more out of the diesel. If this was the case, they were to be disappointed. With just such a vehicle on test, *Safer VW Motoring*'s Chris Burlace reported the performance of the diesel engine to be "virtually indistinguishable" from that of the petrol version. "However, the diesel seemed to produce its power remarkably smoothly ... and the wide, high-torque characteristic served to mask any effect of the extra weight."

The diesel engine weighed some 220lb (100kg) more than its petrol counterpart and it was further held back by the burden of its radiator system and the 16-litres of coolant swilling around inside it. (Kerb weights were respectively 3065lb for the diesel and 2844lb for the 1.6 petrol). Fuel consumption, or the lack of it, could be offered as the 'new' engine's saving grace. Comparing a 1600 petrol engine delivery van to the corresponding diesel, with both running at three-quarters of their respective maximum speeds and at half payload, the petrol version staggered in at 25.6mpg, while the diesel triumphed at 32.8mpg.

The copywriters more or less overlooked the arrival of the diesel engine, at least as far as Europe was concerned. A dismissive "there are now three engines available", which includes "the new 1.6-litre diesel" hardly encouraged queues of would-be buyers. Fortunately, Volkswagen of America took a different stance; even if the overall storyline reproduced at the top of this page was a little suspect. "A diesel powered Vanagon is a natural, because a truly efficient vehicle deserves the most efficient engine. This option points out how thoroughly the Vanagon was designed and engineered."

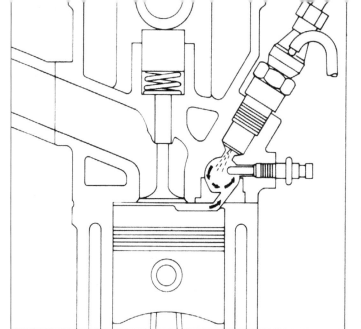

'The spare tire is stored up front in the hinged metal tray. It's accessible by removing just one bolt with the lug wrench.'

3. Technical restructuring – the drip, drip of water

"The Transporter was now fitted with the newly developed water-cooled boxer engines ... Consequently all Volkswagens with the exception of the Beetle had water-cooled engines. This was the conclusion of the technical restructuring." An idea that made history, *VW Public Relations Department, 1991*

The ever-so-bland statement that the arrival of water-cooled engines for the Wedge completed Volkswagen's gigantic "technical restructuring programme", must have been the marketing department's worst nightmare. Undoubtedly it would have had some warning of the impending high tide, even ignoring the start of the progression with the diesel engine. By July 1982, the last air-cooled 2-litre model had left the factory and while the 1600 lingered on for a short time, within months it too had been deleted from the listings. Recall the gurus' words of only a couple of years ago concerning the now defunct, discarded and, by implication, disgraced air-cooled engine. Yes, that's the one that was "renowned for its reliability and durability". Inevitably, brochures designed to shout about the innovations rapidly grew from a tiny trickle to a tidal flood.

"[The water-cooled boxer engine] would carry on the great tradition started by its predecessor," was one attempt to gloss over the usurpation of air-cooled supremacy. After all, the new engines had "high standards in responsiveness and pulling power", exhibited

"maximum economy" and "high acceleration", while "engine noise is much lower too". Warming to the subject, another nail was driven hard into the air-cooled engine's coffin: "Special measures have been taken to cut noise inside the vehicle by 3-4dB (A). The human ear registers this as a 50 per cent noise reduction! The same outstanding results have been obtained for noise levels outside the vehicle. This makes the Transporter, with its water-cooled engine, more pleasant to drive and more acceptable to the environment." The new engine with "driver appeal" demonstrated "another major step forward", for "the water-cooled engine enables the heater to respond more rapidly in cold weather – a blessing for driver and passengers on a winter morning". Following the niceties, air-cooled cremation arrived with the subject of servicing. "The new water-cooled engine cuts costs here too: for example, the first oil change is due only after 5000 miles. The valve gear needs no maintenance, the silencers are of long life pattern ... the clutch needs no routine servicing either." And all because the Wedge had a water-cooled engine.

The new high-pow

With 'technical drawing' outlines on a graph paper background, another launch publication lived up to its scientific look with a slew of statistics: "Over the years, our air-cooled engine has helped make the Transporter the world's best-selling commercial vehicle. No reason, however for us to ignore ways of improving it still further. Retaining its flat-four configuration, therefore we've developed a new water-cooled engine. A powerful combination it is too. 20 per cent more powerful in terms of the petrol version. But more important than that, it now delivers 36 per cent more torque ... Yet for all this extra output, it's a power unit that remains remarkably low-revving. It's no guzzler, either. A more flexibly, evenly balanced engine affording an increase in mpg of up to 15 per cent. Besides being a lot smoother running, you'll also be pleased to hear it's quite a bit quieter."

For Vanagon purchasers in the USA, the copywriters followed suite: "Although the new engine is more compact than its air-cooled predecessor, it's also more powerful – with 22 per cent more horsepower. But the new engine is not all brawn. It has brains, too. A unique 'Digi-Jet' fuel injection system digitally monitors the fuel and air mixture for maximum power output. Just as comforting, the EPA estimates that the new engine is 19 per cent more economical than the old one and 23 per cent more economical on the highway ... Combined with a re-engineered transmission and fully independent suspension, the new engine makes the Vanagon quick and responsive. And a pure joy to drive."

In the first full year of Wedge production (1980), numbers stood at 217,876 to be followed by a lower total of 187,327 the following year and a virtually level 188,681 in 1982, the last when air-cooled engines played a part in the total. Sadly, whatever other advantages the water-cooled engines might have had over their predecessors, boosting sales levels was not one of them. 1983 saw 155,500 Wedges produced, 1984 – 157,596, 1985 – 155,423, 1986 – 161,712, 1987 – 145,380 and so on. Volkswagen's strategy appears to have been to up the spec as much as it could to combat the invasion of similar models from the plants of other manufactures. More engines, splendiferous trim levels, even an off-road, all-wheel drive option for virtually all models raised the stakes certainly, but whether *Car and Driver*'s assessment of the Wedge as the "Porsche 911 of vans" held water is open to question.

ered **Transporters.**

"THE VOLKSWAGEN TRANSPORTER HAS ALWAYS LED THE FIELD IN ADVANCED ENGINEERING, BUT WITH THE NEW WATER-COOLED PETROL ENGINES, THE BENEFITS ARE EVEN GREATER." VW 2/83

Although the 'new' water-cooled engines were just that, there was more than an element of déjà vu to the story. For a start there were two options, one of which demonstrated a more leisurely approach to life than the other – "One carb or two?" asked the salesman, that is unless he was resident in the US, when he would be pontificating about the 'unique digi-jet fuel injection system', on the one gasoline offering. But, of far greater significance, was the fact that here was a unique engine, developed specifically for the Wedge. "The Boxer concept," wrote a remarkably studious copywriter, "with central crankshaft and opposed cylinders, offers

numerous technical advantages and is ideally suited to the Commercial with its direct rear-wheel drive." Both new engines had a cubic capacity of 1913cc, the secret to their respective performance levels being in the number of carburettors. The 60bhp engine, with a 0-50mph time of 19.1secs when coupled to a four-speed box and 18.2 when fitted with the optional five-speed offering, had a single carb. Maximum torque of 103.1lb/ft was achieved at only 2200rpm. Twin carburettors were the key to the extra output of the 78bhp engine. With 0-50mph speeds hacked back to 15.7secs when coupled to a four-speed box, and 15.1 when mated to the

five-speed option, plus a maximum speed of 81mph compared to 73 for the 60bhp option, optimum torque of 103.9lb/ft was achieved at 2600rpm. "The additional output at higher speeds means that the vehicle can be driven at 81mph and over when necessary. This is the ideal power unit for regular runs at high average speeds." Having set the new course, it wasn't all that long before something was done about the leisurely diesel with its top speed of just 68mph and its snail's approach to a 0-50mph sprint of between 24.4secs and 25.7secs (dependent on the number of gears – four or five). For the '86 model year, what better move could there have been than to add a Bosch turbo-charged version of the diesel engine. With a maximum speed of 79mph and

fuel consumption running at 35.7mpg at a constant 56mph, here was something with combined 'oomph' and reasonable economy. "This unit represents a technical advance on the normally aspirated diesel engine, combining two apparently incompatible properties," wrote an ingenious copywriter, "It produces high performance but remains scrupulously economical." To complete the diesel story, in the later years of the Wedge's reign (specifically 1987), the basic engine was up-rated to 57bhp at 4500rpm. Hardly earth shattering, but as the brochure compiler pointed out, here was a favourite for "short journey operation, since its very low fuel consumption minimises operating costs."

4. Getting to grips with the
power of the Wedge

Power boost and syncro – action stations

A multiplicity of options was indicative of exciting, yet challenging times for Volkswagen. Other manufacturers were on the move leaving no room for a nap in the Wolfsburg boardroom. Soon petrol engine options had broken the magic 2000cc barrier, when a 2.1-litre, 112bhp fuel-injected engine hit the road on '86 models and offered a top speed of 94mph. Fast forwarding to 1990 and the last year of the Wedge, this engine was offered in two guises, with and without a 'cat', the former inevitably disadvantaged in terms of performance, producing 92bhp at 4500 rpm. The 78bhp 1900 was also available.

Recalling its aborted four-wheel drive experiment with the Bay during the course of 1985, Volkswagen launched the Transporter in Syncro guise. Having been developed by Steyr-Daimler-Puch, on Volkswagen's behalf, the copywriters had to brush up on the technicalities before they could reveal that the Syncro was "synonymous with latest-technology four-wheel drive ... With automatic distribution of driving power over all four wheels," they added, lest it be forgotten. "The nerve centre of Syncro technology is a viscous coupling which monitors and automatically regulates the additional front wheel drive. Even the slightest difference in speed between the front axle and rear axle – as always occurs even in everyday driving as a result of minimal driving wheel slip – causes the propelling force to be transferred to the front axle gently and smoothly. This means that the four-wheel drive is constantly in operation in virtually all driving situations. There is no switching to be done by the driver as this is not necessary."

Soon available right across the range, the Syncro option proved popular and staved off the approaching legions of competitors for a little bit longer. While brochures produced for the British market were akin to training manuals, in the USA the style was livelier, while also helpful to non-scientists. "The four-wheel drive of the Vanagon GL Syncro 4WD ... is permanent and automatic. It's always there when you need it, engaging smoothly all by itself whenever it senses a difference in speed between the front and rear axles. The Syncro 4WD improves handling in even the foulest of weathers. Provides greater directional control during cornering. And prevents excessive tire scrub. To help you get the most from Syncro 4WD, all models feature an extra low gear for better start-up traction on difficult driving surfaces. Larger tires and higher ground clearance. Plus an 18.4-gallon fuel tank. As a result, the Syncro 4WD adds extra confidence to its already long list of driving pleasures."

CL and GL Caravelle, topped off with the Carat: the executive limousine with space, comfort and performance.

If playing the power game was one course taken by Volkswagen and the addition of off-road capabilities was another, not to mention the choice of a four or five-speed manual and fully automatic gearboxes, then the final cog in the great game of model enhancement for super sales was for the company to offer enhanced fittings – the luxury of deep pile carpets, and sumptuous rich velour. While the Splittie Samba of old might have been but a distant memory, the 'deluxe' Wedges (above the workaday delivery van and Pick-up) joined models such as the Golf and Passat in having a proliferation of badges indicating successively more upmarket levels of trim. Perhaps mention should also be made of the vehicle manufacturer's

well-known device to revitalise stagnant or declining sales ... the limited edition, extra-goodie models at so-called bargain prices.

Re-branding had already led to the more upmarket models being labelled as Caravelles. Aligned to this were three levels of trim. In 1986, for example, the lowliest of the Caravelles, the 'C', was described as "an ideal minibus" and featured "attractive leatherette" and a floor covered in "easily maintained vinyl board". One up was the 'CL', offering "greater luxury in every detail". Apart from "two colour paintwork and chrome trim strips", reversing lights, a lockable glove box, a trip distance recorder and a clock all had their part to play. Of most significance in the pampering department was carpet, which replaced flooring vinyl. At the top of the tree, for the British market at least, was 'the executive bus', the Caravelle GL. "Driver and front passengers relax in anatomically correct executive style seats with velour upholstery," while 'the five seats in the rear ... are splendidly comfortable, with high-quality fabric-covered folding armrests ... there is a heated rear window, rear wash/wipe, a three speed fan and heater, additional insulating material in all doors and side panel trims – in fact, everything to set the Caravelle GL apart."

Starting life as a special limited edition model, the Carat became the flagship model as years went by, remaining so until the Wedge bowed out in all but selected Syncro options in the summer of 1990, just months after the Bus's 40th anniversary celebrations held on March 8th. Here's a snippet from a 1988 brochure, again

printed especially for the British market: "The Carat is pure luxury for six ... Passengers are cosseted in individual cloth seats that have been designed to soak up the miles. The centre seats can be swivelled and locked facing rearwards to provide conference on the move facilities. All seats have their own armrests and individual backrest adjustment. Deep pile carpeting is used throughout ... full air conditioning can be specified ... power steering takes the strain out of parking whilst features such as electrically adjustable heated mirrors and electric windows provide convenience on the move. Externally, the Carat creates a distinctive impression."

As might have been anticipated, the fourth generation Transporter, or T4, was entirely conventional in both its mechanical make-up and the ever-spiralling level of gizmos to dazzle a would-be buyer.

In reality, our story of the Bus more or less ended when the last gasp of air left the Wedge, a point when 21st century ideals, coupled to hefty price tags approaching the £20K mark, intervened. Nevertheless, Volkswagen had created history with its box on wheels, and while the first three generations might be the sought-after models today, no doubt a point will come when both the fourth and fifth generations join the ranks of those vehicles authors wish to write about and readers want to know more about. For the moment even the last of the water-cooled Wedges are on the up in the price stakes, possibly also in an average enthusiast's appreciation ... and rightly so!

1. Staking the pitch – camping it up

A casual observer of the Volkswagen scene over the years might easily have been led to assume that the Camper was one of the standard options in the range, alongside models such as the Kombi and Microbus. After all, and for very good reason, the average Camper bore a striking resemblance to such variants! Although early Splittie brochures lack references to the Camper, by the late 1950s generic offerings often devoted space to "The Volkswagen Camper with Westfalia Deluxe equipment", noting that the vehicle was "a kitchen, bedroom and living room with skylight, curtains, wall-lights and panelled walls". Likewise, many model-specific brochures, be it for a Beetle, Karmann Ghia, or the Splittie itself, would carry an appropriately tantalising message on the back cover: "Why not ask your dealer for information and literature on these other Volkswagen products: VW Pick-up, VW Double cabin Pick-up, VW Delivery Van, VW Kombi, VW Microbus, VW Deluxe Microbus, VW Camper (Westfalia Deluxe equipment), VW Ambulance, VW Karmann Ghia Coupé, VW Karmann Ghia Convertible, VW Industrial Engine?" (*Beetle*, 1959). Turn the page to appreciate exactly what 'literature' was being distributed by dealers. In the 1960s the same message was perpetuated, as neatly illustrated by the cleverly contrived photograph that adorns this page, taken from a brochure bearing the date '8/63'.

However, the truth of the matter remains that Volkswagen did not manufacture a Camper. The concept was not its own; instead the notion of utilising models in the Splittie line-up for holiday or weekend-away usage was the brainchild of Westfalia, the coach building company which was based at Rheda-Wiedenbrück in the state of Rhine-Westfalia. The radically different Splittie had galvanised Westfalia into action at a time when the relaxation of postwar austerity measures meant leisure time pursuits were both sought and, at last, affordable. The Splittie, through Westfalia's initiative, became synonymous with camping activities and a myriad of other converters were soon eager to join the bandwagon. Volkswagen and Westfalia remained loyal to each other – checkout the Vanagon Camper to confirm the enduring nature of the relationship as far as the first 40 years of Buses are concerned. A limited number of other companies however were recognised by Volkswagen and nominated as official converters. All had to satisfy Volkswagen that, particularly with the insertion of an elevating roof, they were doing nothing that would affect the Buses rigidity. The selection of companies featured over the next 20-plus pages includes pioneers, officially nominated converters and one or two of the more way-out and less successful operations.

2. Westfalia Wanderers

THE VOLKSWAGEN CAMPER

WITH WESTFALIA DE LUXE EQUIPMENT

VW – the Volkswagen Camper with Westfalia deluxe equipment

With company origins dating back to 1844, the name Westfalia was officially registered in 1922. By the 1930s, having patented a trailer hitch ball, the company was manufacturing caravan and camping trailers. Hefty to say the least, wealthy owners required cars such as the latest Mercedes models to tow them. Although the Westfalia factory was badly bomb damaged during the war, the company crawled back into action exhibiting its first steel-plate caravan at the Hanover Fair in 1947. By the end of the decade it was also producing trailers specifically designed for use in conjunction with the Beetle. With little more than 12 months Splittie production under Volkswagen's belt, Westfalia introduced its so-called Camping Box in April 1951, literally a removable wooden cabinet that slotted neatly width-ways behind the passenger compartment. Suitable for use with all the Splittie variants available at the time, it possibly gained most favour with Kombi owners. Spartan in the extreme, the 'box' consisted of little more than a fold-down bed and two drawers. Slowly but surely additional items were added including a wardrobe (not necessarily of a hanging nature – think folding for once!), a large wooden cupboard attached to one of the double side-doors, a petrol- or spirit-burning cooker and a useful awning. It was March 1953 before the first price list emerged, indicating the Camping Box with "four high-quality cushions" cost 595 DM, while the wash and shave unit was priced at 62.5 DM. Revolutionary and inspirational the Camping Box might have been, but it took several years before the 1000th, and by this time potentially more sophisticated unit, had been sold. In 1958, Westfalia opened a Camper assembly line leading to publication of brochures like the one reproduced here.

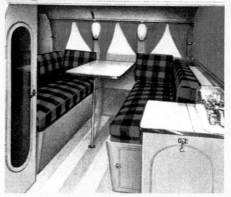
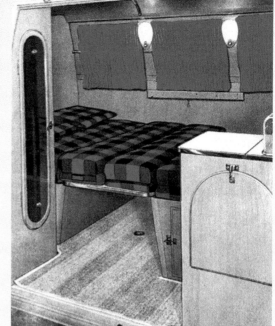

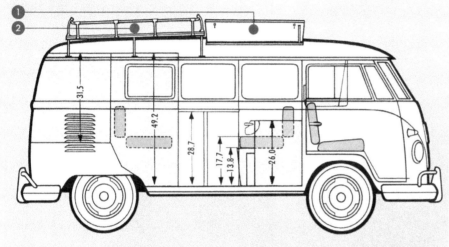

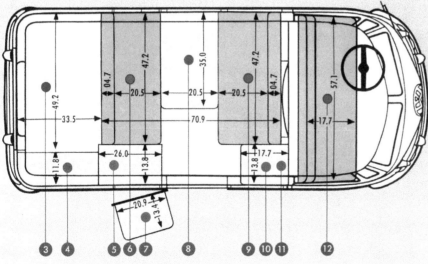

1 Skylight
2 Roof rack
3 Luggage area
4 Double door cupboard
5 Wardrobe
6 Rear bench
7 Flap for cooker
8 Large folding table
9 Front bench
10 Kitchen/washroom cabinet
11 Fitted beakers
12 Beds for two children

"It's the handsomest home-in-a-station-wagon you ever did see."

By the end of the 1950s, Westfalia was firmly established as makers of camper conversions for the Splittie. Volkswagen's marketing men were hard at work on their behalf too, not only giving the product the hard sell, but also pointing out the "useful" optional extras that were available such as "this cupboard with a 2 cubic feet icebox on the right and storage compartment on the left. Under the roof of the car the luggage net takes all those little odds and ends you want to keep handy." Information tripped lightly off the tongue: "The 23-gallon water tank with its electric pump is fitted inside the front bench and still leaves room for other gear alongside which can be reached by lifting the seat, or through the side flap ... Two further convenient extras [are stowed here too]: a two-ring gasoline cooker and a portable chemical toilet."

As for the main sell, considering that DDB wasn't quite yet in on the act, the text was remarkably lively: "You have a yen to travel to off-beat places, but aren't sure about the accommodation? You'd love an outdoor holiday, but want your comfort too? Want to roam, but like a homely feeling? The Volkswagen Camper is for you! It's not just a converted sedan – and you don't have to tow a heavy, cumbersome trailer either ... it's the handsomest home-on-a-station wagon you ever did see. Did we say 'Station Wagon?' ... well name it what you will – there's just nothing around to compare it with. ... Take a look inside! You'll marvel at the ingenuity, the forethought that have gone into planning your comfort, right down to the minutest detail ... No need to travel light if you've got a Volkswagen camper! Anything else you wish for your convenience? ... a tent perhaps? We've thought of that too. All along one side of the vehicle goes a gaily striped awning to form a porch."

By 1962, the marketing men were posing a question: "Which body types make good campers?" Their answer: "These four (besides the VW Camper). The VW Panel Truck. The VW Kombi Station Truck. The VW Deluxe Station Wagon. The VW Standard Station Wagon."

Motor Trend tested the 'Volkswagen Kamper' for itself as far back as 1956. "More of a way of life than just another car, the VW Bus, when completely equipped with the ingenious German-made Kamper kit, can open up new vistas of freedom (or escape) from a humdrum life. ... When you stop for the night, you'll find that the Kamper's planners did quite a job with a minimum of fanfare. The interior is deceptively simple: just the folding table, a little folding bench beside it on one side and a plaid-covered, full length bench with seat and back cushions on the other ... everything is at hand."

"Want to get away from it all? Then you should look into our Volkswagen Campmobile."

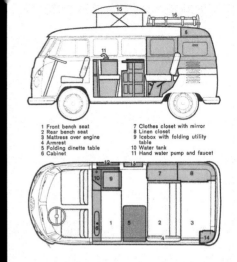

1 Front bench seat
2 Rear bench seat
3 Mattress over engine
4 Armrest
5 Folding dinette table
6 Cabinet
7 Clothes closet with mirror
8 Linen closet
9 Icebox with folding utility table
10 Water tank
11 Hand water pump and faucet

Floor covering and rug

Drapes for all windows in living compartment

Rod and drapes between the driver's cab and living compartment

Electric circuit

Three 2½-gallon water canisters, stowed in the chest underneath the front bench

Hammock for child's sleeping accommodation

Skylight (35.8in L x 20.9in W)

Roof rack: (53in L x 56in W x 18in H, 220lb payload)

Drop-leaf table at left-hand door wing for stove

Large side tent with poles and attachments

Chemical toilet

Two-burner gasoline stove.

Some of the suggestions seem more dated than others: "Want more headroom in your Campmobile? Then you should order our optional pop-up top with screened windows. Lets all the cigarette smoke out and lots of fresh air in."

In 1962, the powers that be at Volkswagen of America were sufficiently 'enthusiastic' about the whole Camping scene to organise what amounted to a glorified price list of the many options available. Ranging from $399 to $1088, the complete package listings make interesting reading.

West B-33 ($1088)

Interior side and roof panelling with birch plywood; the motor compartment has a

Plastic covering

Wardrobe with inside mirror

Linen closet

Ice box

Washing cabinet with wash bowl at right-hand door wing

Folding table attached to frame between the two benches

Two benches (front and rear) with removable seat cushions and back rests converting into double bed

Two wedge shaped headrests

Today, it's your second car... but tomorrow, or next weekend

With the arrival of the Bay, business really boomed for Westfalia, especially in the USA; 30,000 conversions based on the Splittie or Bay had been sold since the days of the first Camping Boxes by March 1968. Just three years later that number had risen to 100,000!

"This house was made for living."

"The basis for the 1968 Campmobile is VW's bus-type station wagon which teams attractive new looks this year with a number of major mechanical improvements ... Two major options are available for the 1968 VW Campmobile. One is a 'pop-top' which literally raises the roof, providing more standing space inside as well as a luggage rack and child's upper berth on top. The other major option is a free-standing tent which quickly can add a fully-enclosed 9ft 8in by 6ft 6in room alongside the vehicle." *Foreign Car Guide*, Feb 1968.

"In a Campmobile you don't have to pass the scenery by. You drive right into it."

By the 1970s, if a purchaser wished to read something inspirational about a Westfalia Camper, the best place to turn was to the USA. While the specification details of the Campmobile were carefully listed towards the end of each brochure, the images, like the one reproduced here, were stunning, while the text had a certain DDB zing to it.

"The Campmobile windows are all giant-sized, side and rear. The windshield is one piece to give you a commanding view of the road as well as the scenery around you. And nobody is in a better position to watch out for the other guy. The ones in front. And the ones behind."

The tent illustrated above even got its own bit of marketing speak, DDB style. "The Campmobile tent, while not standard, has to be one of the most desirable items ever offered. Specifically designed for the Campmobile in the way it sets up and stores, it adds lots of precious space. The tent has its own floor and is firmly free-standing. Drive away for the day if you like. The tent will hold what you won't need for your day's excursion, while holding your spot for your return.'

With the emergence of the Bay, Westfalia's pop-up-top arrangements improved drastically. The copywriter, in reference manual mode, enlightened would-be purchasers thus: "The pop-up fibreglass top and luggage rack. Provides extra head-room. Three screened openings with flaps for extra ventilation. Roof includes 5ft canvas cot for one more child. Luggage rack contains buffer rods and tie-down hooks. Can be reached from within the pop-up top."

'THE COMFORTS OF HOME AND THE RIDE OF A CAR'

Back in 1971 when the 100,000th Westfalia Camper conversion hit the highway, everything in the garden appeared rosy. Sadly, the oil crisis of 1973 hit hard, with US market sales, for example, tumbling by as much as 35 per cent virtually overnight. While such depressed levels of sales were relatively short lived, a feeling prevailed that, almost like Volkswagen and the Bay, Westfalia had lost some interest, despite the introduction of both the Helsinki and Berlin models. However, the birth of the Wedge in 1979, christened a new Camper generation, marketed as the 'Joker'.

The marketing men highlighted some of the plus points with due hype. The "quest for perfection in a mobile kitchenette shows up in the swivel tables that convert from counter tops to dining tables." Sections of the motoring press were equally happy to write with gusto and praise.

"The Vanagon Westfalia camper is probably the neatest, most compact camper conversion available in vans today. Elegant inside or out, there's genius in every drawer."

By September 1984, Westfalia had successfully completed its 250,000th conversion since the days of the primitive Camping Boxes, which had started it all. A last word reserved for the marketing men. To demonstrate the luxurious nature of the Wedge-based Campmobile, the copywriter had a novel approach: "Your Camper can be air-conditioned and an automatic transmission is available. Otherwise your options are limited, because we tried to think of everything you might want to add – and made it not just standard, but special. When we made the Vanagon Camper we made it as versatile as possible and there's only one way to do it. Completely."

153

Pioneering an open-plan Moto-Caravan

Peter Pitt, an Austrian refugee, was a pioneering converter of Splitties into campers in Britain. The first such vehicles were produced in 1956, but all was not straightforward as the Splittie was considered to be a commercial vehicle and its top speed, therefore, summarily restricted to a miserable 30mph. Pitt deliberately drove through the Royal Park at Windsor, a place where such vehicles were banned, but the publicity generated and his subsequent trial had the desired effect, with the result that his 'Moto-Caravan' was classed as a private car and free to travel at more realistic speeds. Sadly, import duties still helped to restrict sales of the Volkswagen, making it more expensive than homegrown products such as the Ford Thames and Commer 1500.

Business conference and family recreation, or dining table for four.

As the cover illustration reproduced from the 1966 Moto-Caravan brochure clearly indicates not only had Peter Pitt been taken over by Canterbury Sidecars, but also all conversion work had been transferred to South Ockenden in Essex. The change had occurred in 1961, at a time when Pitt was in the process of refining his original offering.

Pitt's design arrangements had always been versatile, albeit with a height restriction thanks to the lack of any form of pop-up top (although an optional loft, somewhat precariously balanced on the solid roof could be specified). Early brochures proclaimed that "unique features" gave "over thirty 'easy to arrange' layouts", while "any of the various arrangements [could] be made in 1½ minutes." Perhaps the most contrived marketing material related to the Camper's suitability as "the conference home away from home". "Spacious comfort for the living requirements of the 'man on the road' brings the daily expenses into shillings in place of pounds. 1½ minutes rearrangement gives you a perfect conference table and seating to entertain and conduct your business in your own surroundings. Luggage space to take 16 average suit or sample cases is provided."

Of the genuinely inspirational, here's the best: "Tastefully designed interiors – prosperous setting in colours of your choice. Precision built by craftsmen to a fine degree of accuracy – each piece fully interlocking for re-arrangement without need for screws or bolts. Highest quality Dunlopillo foam rubber cushions and mattresses and hard scratch-proof Formica tops."

155

'Take a good look' Bay brochure, Oct 1968

By 1966, not only had an elevating roof been added as an optional extra to the standard package for all models, but also the list of variations between specifications had developed. Although the Kombi was 'now completely trimmed', it was still the cheapest conversion in its base form, rolling in at £210 10s 0d when accommodating two adults and two children (kit and vehicle, with its "'new 1500cc engine", cost £939). The Deluxe Microbus conversion however, cost £241, or £1248 with the vehicle price tagged in. It was nevertheless easy to erode the difference by adding to the Kombi's specification. For example, a fold away cooker and "griller in cabinet on side door with grill pan, two-ring", a standard part of the more luxurious model's package, cost an additional £8 18s 6d as an "adjustment in lieu of the ordinary two-ring cooker". As for the elevating roof "with two roof bunks, rear skylight and one-piece PVC side walls", that cost £110, no matter what model it was fitted to. However, decide to have such a kit fitted retrospectively and then the cost rose by £5 to £115. To complicate issues a little, customers could decide to have an elevating roof fitted minus the bunks. "If roof

bunks not required, allow £15," advised the helpful copywriter.

Inevitably with the arrival of the Bay, Canterbury, through Peter Pitt, set about designing a revised layout to accommodate the new vehicle's attributes, chief of which was a sliding door. The cooker which had graced the Splitties hinge-opening double doors for so long was now relocated to the bulkhead, while arrangements were made to swing it out to be used outside. By October 1968, a fully kitted out Microbus Bay, but without an elevating roof, cost £1195 8s 0d, having previously retailed at £1180 8s 0d at launch, compared to the final Splittie versions of this model, which had cost £1025. Sadly, Peter Pitt died in February 1969 and, although Canterbury continued to churn out conversions based on models other than the Volkswagen, Pitt's designs for Bay expired with him as they had been manufactured under licence.

"Space for everything, specialist designed, craftsman constructed. Discover the comfort of living in this luxuriously appointed all new Canterbury Moto-Caravan – a new concept in mobile home design." 1968 Bay brochure.

the
NEW
CANTERBURY
OPEN PLAN works so well…

4. "You can't appreciate Devon in a day."

To many, a Volkswagen-based Camper conversion is synonymous with the name Devon. The first Splittie conversions appeared in 1956 as the result of a 'partnership' between soon-to-be national distributor, Lisburne Garage of Babbacombe Road in Torquay and the long established Sidmouth-based cabinet making firm of J P White, whose responsibility it was to both design and produce the range. Over the years the emphasis changed with the White name becoming prominent, followed by a name change to Devon Conversions Ltd (member of the RWD Group), then relocation in the early days of the Wedge to Exeter. Towards the end of the period covered here, Devon faltered and only a management buyout saved the day.

During the Splittie era the range blossomed from a straightforward Caravette, which, although it for some years lacked an elevating roof, nevertheless provided a good level of creature comforts for the time, to a 'Devonette', "designed to meet the requirements of those seeking a high quality Motor Caravan at a more economic price". By the time the 1500 engine Splittie was established, the Caravette could be specified as either a 'Standard' model, or as a 'Spaceway'. "This new version of the Devon Caravette provides a feature which will appeal to many people, in that access is available from the cab without the need to go outside the vehicle. The conversion thereby takes on a different form and its unique feature is the special unit comprising a two-burner cooker with grill, 7-gallon water tank with pump, bottled gas storage and

useful drawer." At the same time an "entirely new conversion", the Torvette, was launched, again available as both a standard or Spaceway conversion, but designed to "provide a lower priced model of exceptionally high quality."

Devon's copywriter in 1966 was sufficiently confident in the Caravette to proclaim: "It's a busy life and the Devon thrives on it. Look what it gives you – a craftsman-built conversion on the Volkswagen Microbus comprising – seating for eight on deep foam cushions with zip-on 'Duracour' covers – comfortable double bed for two adults and singles for two children – two-burner gas cooker with grill – built in 7-gallon water tank with swivel pump and polythene bowl – extra 2-gallon plastic water container – two tables, both adaptable for outdoor use – 'Easicool' evaporation food cooler – 'Gaydon' melamine crockery and stainless steel cutlery for four persons – built in fluorescent lighting – 6ft 6in square side awning in lightweight Continental canvas – large storage space – curtains for all windows on nylon runners and alloy rails – hardwearing floor surface – all interior fabrics and surfaces in choice of colours – plus the renowned Devon natural-oak woodwork."

Fully approved by Volkswagenwerk, Wolfsburg, W. Germany
Volkswagen Motors Ltd., Volkswagen Concessionaires for Great Britain.

"THE HOLIDAY MAKERS – DEVON MOTOR CARAVANS MAKE EVERY WEEKEND A HOLIDAY."

The arrival of the Bay, and a general growth in the market, allowed Devon to spread its wings with a wider variety of models. In 1969 the top of the range Eurovette cost £1338 and was described as the vehicle for "discriminating people who want the best. It has everything for the enthusiast and comfort enough to tempt the most pampered city dweller back to nature." The Caravette, at £1238, offered "the same high quality craftsmanship but fewer standard fittings initially", while the Torvette, based on the Kombi (unlike the other conversions, which utilised the Microbus) was allegedly "becoming Britain's most popular motorised caravan conversion." At £1138 perhaps it was easy to see why.

Within a couple of years, a new top of the range model had appeared, while the higher specification conversion was also available on the lower spec model, the Kombi. Prices ranged from £1433 for the Moonraker based on the Microbus down to £1275 for the Sunlander Kombi. Brochures designed and produced around this time were amongst the best. Here's a conscientious copywriter on the subject of the Moonraker: "With many additional refinements for the discriminating motor-caravanner, the Moonraker offers the ultimate in luxury. The cab seats three and two forward-facing seats, one of which reverses for dining, accommodate a further four people. A simple re-arrangement of the seating provides luxurious sleeping accommodation for two adults and two children."

VW Devon MOONRAKER

Amazingly, by 1976, Devon was offering customers a Westfalia model as part of its line-up. Branded as the VW Continental, while the West German company's name wasn't mentioned, there was an open admission that the vehicle was 'imported'. Perhaps even more surprisingly the vehicle's description left no doubt that here was a 'luxury motor caravan'. With inflation rampant, the lowest-priced offering, a Devonette standard model based on the 1600cc Panelvan, rolled in at £3125.87 inclusive of the dreaded VAT. A 2000cc engine added £243.75 to the price, an automatic box an additional £229.67. This was February, by October 20th the same vehicle retailed at £3792.88. As for the Westfalia, sorry Continental, that vehicle came in at a staggering £5764, a price not all that far short of a very different conversion: the all-singing and dancing Devon water-cooled LT 28 HI-TOP, which nearly commanded £7000 (£6,997.68). Perhaps Devon's proudest claim at the time was to be "the only official VW converters".

By 1978 it was all change again, with the top model being a "brand new motor caravan" built on the Kombi and branded 'Moonraker', while the equally new Sundowner was based on the Panelvan. The theme for both models was of comfortable beds, more cupboard space and water storage, luxury trim and even a louvre window.

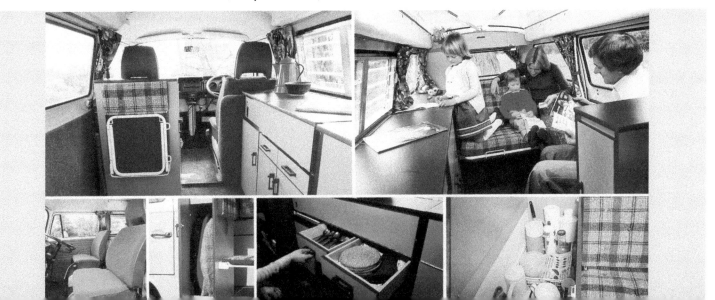

VW Devon Wedges

The emergence of the Wedge seemed to coincide with a ham marketing strategy at Devon. Perhaps indicative of the latest whims in design and marketing, but hopefully not, the storyline was of the "ingredients" required to create the perfect Camper recipe. Perhaps those with knowledge of the English Lake District might have been a little put off by the decidedly foreign looking picture used to depict this most popular of locations! Prices for the 1600cc Moonraker based on the Kombi, and complete with a Double Top roof, came out at £7658.33.

"Method. Take one Devon Moonraker and add to it the following ingredients: first, make the seating deliciously comfortable and adaptable. Add a tastefully designed kitchen and storage unit. Blend with a generous helping of luxury. An elevating roof that rises beautifully. Fill with sleeping arrangements designed for really sweet dreams. Add a dash of style."

An unbeatable combination

An unbeatable combination?

The extra oomph of 112bhp petrol engines and turbo-diesel offerings suggested that Devon would keep its conversions up-to-date in terms of mid-1980s aspirations, which indeed it had. According to the copywriter, all three ranges were "well worth a closer look". From the Eurovette pictured third from the left above, allegedly "the ultimate in design and luxury" to the Caravette, "one of the best value for money vehicles on the road today", (second left) and the "firm favourite", the Moonraker, depicted both with and without a Hi-Top roof, the fittings were both comprehensive and of modern appearance. While Devon's once renowned cabinet-style furniture might have given way to "doors framed in solid wood", and "luxurious woodgrain laminates", there were gimmicks offered as compensation, including "cab seats re-trimmed to match the saloon seats" and individual reading lights over the bed.

Safer VW Motoring magazine commented of the Wedge Moonraker that it "continues to be a well designed and constructed conversion". The tester, Chris Burlace, liked the way that "the storage space is at all times accessible ... the kitchen unit is arranged in a practical manner ... seating is comfortable ... the beds are quick to arrange [and the] cushions of the lower bed [had] just the right degree of firmness."

5. The dandy Danbury

Whatever else they achieved, for many years the firm that borrowed the name of the place where its conversions were built, namely Danbury near Chelmsford in Essex, managed to release some of the most basic and un-inspirational literature imaginable. Perhaps realistically this was a result of the decision to concentrate on a modular equipment approach, which tended to create a less than extensively furnished van. Browsing through promotional literature dating from the early and later 1970s, the specification seemed to change little. (Danbury stopped using Volkswagens as a basis for its conversions in 1972, returning to the fold in 1977.) Within the passenger, or living area, of the Danbury the "two forward lockers slide back and lock in a forward-facing travelling position", and when parked they could be adapted to form part of an "L-shaped day settee". Meals were prepared via "the Danbury high-pressure cooker" which was "functional, super efficient" and could be swung down "into the front locker when not in use ... thus creating another seat for that extra traveller." To be blunt, the arrangements were a tad primitive, while prices were slightly dearer than those charged for the better-equipped Devon models. A Kombi conversion in 1970 rolled in at £1200, while a Microbus cost a further £50. An elevating roof sent the bill up by a further £120.

The Motor tested a Danbury in the dying days of the Splittie, at a time when the conversion cost from £983 upwards. What would undoubtedly be slated today was heartily condoned the best part of 40 years ago. Apart from praising the "various seating arrangements" and noting that it was possible "to seat up to seven adults around the large free standing table provided", the writer delighted in the available space to bed down snoring youngsters, as well as the "considerable space" to locate bedding, cooking utensils and clothing.

Optional extras in 1970 consisted of an "elevating roof with two adult bunks", which could be fitted for £120, large cushions at £2 5s 0d each, half cushions at £1 10s 0d and a child's stretcher bunk in the cab, which amounted to £12 10s 0d. Filler boards, perhaps appropriately, were the only other accessory, and cost £1 0s 0d each.

Danbury

With the emergence of the Wedge, Danbury continued to produce simple literature to match the style of its conversions. Then, in 1981, a brochure appeared that transformed the look. Reproduced here, it followed closely the style of Volkswagen's own offerings for the European markets and even included familiar photographs of the new 'model'. Danbury had something to shout about too – "The new Volkswagen Danbury Series 11 lets you travel in style." Here was the "first-ever motorised caravan to have an electrically-operated fully automatic elevating roof". The marketing men went to town. This was no longer a semi-amateur piece of print. "The Volkswagen Danbury Series 11 is a quality motor caravan that has been superbly designed to give you maximum comfort and versatility. It's generous in space, tasteful in décor, ideal for relaxing or dining in and packed with thoughtful fitments to make life easy. Just at a push of a button, the 'Autoroof' elevates silently to almost double the interior space, as well as to give full standing room. By simply sliding the centre front-facing chair/locker forward and flipping the backrest, the cabin becomes a lounge …'. The list of goodies that followed was generous and included a "stainless steel two-burner with a Camping Gaz grill … an excellent stainless steel sink/draining board … a super deluxe spacious Electrolux refrigerator … 12-volt television socket … and a lockable electrical cupboard".

During a troubled period for Camper conversion firms in the 1980s, many 'names' fell, some of which never re-appeared. Danbury was one that hit the rocks, but the name re-appeared many years later, even offering conversions of the Brazilian produced Bay until that model's demise in 2005.

At last, a genuine Dandy D!

6. Calling at Moortown, Caraversions and more

The Moortown Autohome range

Moortown Motors Ltd. Regent Street, Leeds 2 Tel 31894

The list of companies offering camping conversions on Splitties, Bays and Wedges is almost endless, although the number that survived throughout the period covered by this book can be counted on one hand. While the USA was Volkswagen's most important export market for many a year, it was also the country most closely tied to Westfalia after Germany itself, with plenty of literature encompassing the Campmobile as an integral part of the family. Nevertheless, other US operations sold conversions with some success. In Britain the camper movement was particularly strong as has already been demonstrated.

The aim in the remaining pages is to make at least passing reference to some of the big names not already touched on, while also covering one or two of what might best be regarded as the also rans.

Anyone familiar with Volkswagen's distributor and dealer network in Britain in the 1950s and '60s would recognise the name Moortown Motors as a prominent player in the north of England. However, there was another string to the company's bow with the conversion of both Kombis and Microbuses to Campers under the Autohome brand. Perhaps surprisingly, for a time Moortown also converted both Ford and Standard models, but this came to an end in the spring of 1961. By 1962, Moortown was offering two conversions, known respectively as the Mark 1B and the Mark 5. The 1B's basic equipment included "a two-burner calor gas cooker unit, washbasin, water storage containers, full-length wardrobe, spacious storage lockers, fitted crockery cupboard and curtains to all windows".

Interestingly all the cabinetwork was finished in "polished Jap oak", while "horizontal surfaces ... were 'Formica-topped'". Floors were "lino-tiled throughout". The main distinguishing feature of the Mk 5 was its separate front seats for the driver and passenger, compared to the traditional bench of the Mark 1B. As Moortown's text writer commented, the new seats gave "the designers considerable scope for a variation in the interior layout".

As an optional extra, incurring a surcharge of £100, the Autohome models could be fitted with the 'Calthorpe Elevating Roof', to modern eyes a monstrous affair of almost unequalled ugliness! "The roof is elevated in seconds by one simple movement on an easy roller operation, providing an interior height of 6ft 3in over a considerable floor area ... Of metal coach-built construction, the Calthorpe Elevating Roof forms an integral part of the body."

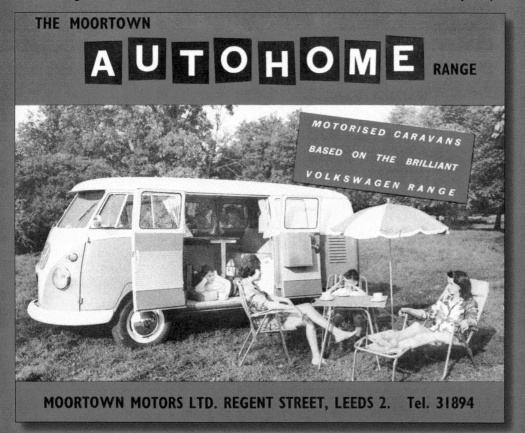

THE MOORTOWN AUTOHOME RANGE

MOTORISED CARAVANS BASED ON THE BRILLIANT VOLKSWAGEN RANGE

MOORTOWN MOTORS LTD. REGENT STREET, LEEDS 2.   Tel. 31894

HiTop
on the Volkswagen by
CARAVERSIONS
lexham gardens mews W.8.

While most manufacturers offered some sort of elevating roof at an additional cost over and above that of their various conversions, Caraversions went one step further with its HiTop model, a hideous arrangement with as much aesthetic charm as an upturned bath welded to the roof of a passing Rolls Royce. Precariously vulnerable to the gentlest of breezes, the overall height of the vehicle was 8ft 2in. Despite being amazingly well appointed and relatively attractively priced at £1190, it remains unsurprising that not many HiTops were sold.

Coachbuilders Martin Walter solved the problem of the provision of an elevating roof for many manufacturers. With origins stretching as far back as the 1770s, by the early 1950s the Kentish operation was dabbling in the motor-home business. Out of this was born the Dormobile name and while Volkswagen conversions did eventually play a relatively small part in Martin Walter's product range, the ingenious design of its elevating roof was sufficient alone to make the company's name famous in Volkswagen circles. The roof was constructed out of fibreglass with two skylights cut into it, while collapsible stripy side skirts were made of particularly hard wearing plastic. Devon charged customers £118 for the Martin Walter Elevating Roof without bunks in 1966, but pointed out in its literature that the roof provided "additional sleeping accommodation for two adults and by day [gave] full-standing-headroom". Although Volkswagen frowned on manufacturers that jeopardised the structural rigidity of the Splittie, VW Motors in London seemed to have little hesitation in promoting the Dormobile and particularly the Martin Walter Elevating Roof.

"The sturdy glass fibre Dormobile roof opens in seconds to give over 8ft headroom above the central living area and two 5ft 11in roof bunks fold down from the canopy. If the children are ready for bed – then you can be left in the peace of your own berth below." 1968 Dormobile Caravan brochure.

E-Z Camper

AMERICA'S MOST POPULAR SPORT

E-Z Camper and America's most popular sport

While the US market was dominated by Westfalia conversions, other manufacturers weren't entirely dormant. E-Z Campers was based at Littlerock, California and produced what it described as a "beautiful, practical, versatile, compact" camper. The specification was certainly attractive and include "diamondized polyclad plywall interiors, 50lb capacity ice box in coppertone, old copper finish forged iron hardware, five safety glass windows aluminum screened, two-burner gasoline stove, easy to clean vinyl floor tile on top of tempered masonite, 54in x 108in awning with side curtains, Husky 6ft 2in bed with 4in plyafoam mattress, folding tables with

Sportsmobile

THE "FAMILY WAGON CAMPER" FOR VOLKSWAGENS

genuine 'Nevamar' tops trimmed in chrome and a 12 gall Calif. code approved water system with pump". The price at the start of the 1960s – $2895.

"Sportsmobile, just the right size," so said manufacturers Andrews of Indiana. Described as "outstanding" by *World Car Guide* magazine in May 1968, the conversions based on the new Bay model could be ordered either in kit form, or complete through "some participating VW dealers". Sportsmobile went on to offer a whole series of different conversions each offering what, at the time, was considered the height of fashionable good taste options. Here's a brief extract covering the Clubcar's sofa-like rear seat: "Soft, quiet, luxurious comfort everywhere you go! Clubcar's rear seat is comfort designed. Steel frame with springs, 3in firm foam topped with 2.5in soft stratafiber with glove soft fabric backed vinyl means 'super comfort'. Soft, fiber-filled bolsters add to your lounging pleasure. Back cushion locks in two positions – upright, or lounge. Headrest swings down, for coach effect, when desired."

HOLDSWORTH Ⓥ VOLKSWAGEN

With Volkswagen's Bus aspirations in the hands of the Wedge, the market for Camper conversions seemed as healthy as ever. By this time in Britain three firms had been granted 'official' conversion status for their products: Autohomes, Autosleepers and Richard Holdsworth.

In 1967 Holdsworth had started converting both new and used Volkswagens, while also providing kits for those who preferred to do it themselves. Business prospered and within 12 months the company had moved to new, larger premises at Woodley, near Reading in Berkshire. By 1976 its most expensive conversion based on the 1600 Bay and complete with a 'Weathershields' elevating roof cost £3419.17. In the days of the early water-cooled Wedges, Holdsworth was offering the Villa 3 with a choice of three different roof forms, plus the Vision, a conversion using the Volkswagen's high top model, which it felt took some beating for "sheer interior space and outstanding features in relationship to exterior size".

Autosleepers broke away from its original policy of producing conversions based just on Commers in 1971, while in 1977 it was the first British company to offer a coach-built model. Nowhere has it been suggested that the Cotswold-based company had particular leanings to the Volkswagen range, although its Hi-top conversion of the mid-1980s luxuriated in high quality, well-designed fittings. Autosleepers was sufficiently confident in the product that it was able to say that "the inside has to be seen to be believed – it is superb." As for the exterior, the superlative used was "eye-catching", going on to elaborate that "not only is there an attractive paint scheme with contrasting coachlines, but the wheel trims, roof rack and ladder are fitted as standard".

Following the spiral into receivership of the giant CI group at the start of 1983, the company was split up and the Autohomes subsidiary sold off to former CIA directors. Renamed Autohomes UK Ltd, but still based at Poole in Dorset, the company produced three conversions based on the early water-cooled Wedge, respectively named the Kamper, Kameo and Karisma, with the last mentioned model being at the top of the range specification. Both the Kameo and the Karisma were specifically designed with two people occupancy in mind.

List of featured brochures

Bibliography

Fifty years of Ice Cream Vehicles, Whitby&Earnshaw, Trans-Pennine Publishing, 1999
Home away from Home – The World of Camper Vans and Motorhomes, Kate Trant, Black Dog Publishing, 2005
Motorhomes The Illustrated History, Andrew Jenkinson, Veloce, 2003
Original VW Bus, Laurence Meredith, MBI Publishing, 1997
Remember those great Volkswagen ads?, David Abbott & Alfredo Marcantonio, European Illustration, 1982
Small Wonder, Walter Henry Nelson, Hutchinson &Co, 1970
The VW Story, Jerry Sloniger, Patrick Stephens, 1980
Volkswagen Bus Camper Van '54-'67, R M Clarke, Brooklands Books
Volkswagen Bus Camper Van '54-'67, R M Clarke, Brooklands Books
Volkswagen Bus Camper Van '54-'67, R M Clarke, Brooklands Books,
Volkswagen Chronicle Vol 7, Group Communications, Volkswagen AG, 2003
Volkswagen History to Hobby, Bob Cropsey, Jersey Classic Publishing, 2004
Volkswagen Model History, Joachim Kuch, Haynes Publishing, 1999
Volkswagen The air-cooled era in colour, Richard Copping, Veloce , 2005
Volkswagen Transporter, Laurence Meredith, Crowood Press, 1998
VW Bus Camper Van Pick-up, Malcolm Bobbitt, Veloce, 1997
VW Campingwagen, Michael Steinke, Schrader Verlag, 2003
VW Transporter/Bus 1949 -1967, Walter Zeichner, Schiffer, 1989
VW Transporter & Microbus Specification Guide – 1950 to 1967, David Eccles, Crowood Press, 2002

Volkswagen – The Air-cooled Era in Colour

ISBN: 978-1-787111-21-9

A vibrant, picture-led chronicle of the Volkswagen story through the '50s and '60s, making extensive use of the artwork from contemporary promotional literature for a real retro feel.

VELOCE
Classic Reprints

Volkswagen Camper –

40 years of freedom: an A-Z of popular Camper conversions

ISBN: 978-1-787111-22-6

VW Buses command a massive following – with Campers the most popular of all. Complementing the author's successful volume covering the first three generations of Volkswagen's legendary Transporter, this book delves exclusively into the spin-off conversions based on the VW Panelvan, Kombi and Microbus that have become known simply as VW Campers. Based on original marketing material, this unique style of presenting the complete story of the Volkswagen-based Camper phenomenon reproduces each company's original sales literature, replacing the original text with a fascinating history written by a knowledgeable enthusiast. Packed with original marketing images, including unusual, discontinued models ,this book will fascinate any VW fanatic.

Also from Veloce Publishing ...

A unique volume dedicated to three generations of the legendary VW Transporter. Meticulously researched with many model specific photographs reproduced to illustrate a genuinely informative text.

ISBN: 978-1-845840-22-8
Paperback • 19.5x13.9cm
• 64 pages

The complete practical guide to modifying classic to modern VW Bus (Transporter) T1 to T5 suspension, brakes and chassis for maximum performance. Contains essential information on using aftermarket parts and interchangeable parts from other production vehicles to achieve great handling (and a lower stance if required).

ISBN: 978-1-845842-62-8
Paperback • 25x20.7cm • 144 pages

For more information and price details, visit our website at www.veloce.co.uk

• email: info@veloce.co.uk • Tel: +44(0)1305 260068

THE CAMPER CONVERSION MANUAL™

How to convert Volkswagen
T5
VAN
to CAMPER

Lindsay Porter

Covers all Volkswagen T5 (2003 on) short-wheelbase Panel Van & Window Van models. Useful for Shuttle, Caravelle & long-wheelbase models. Covers all engine & transmission types, plus Automatic & 4Motion

Convert your own VW panel van to a Camper, and you've got the best of all worlds, as the author of this manual shows. A detailed step-by-step guide with 1500 illustrations, covering every aspect of the conversion: you save a fortune, learn a lot, and get a great recreational vehicle! Covers T5 models 2003 on.

ISBN: 978-1-904788-67-6
Paperback • 27x20.7cm • 272 pages

THE CAMPER CONVERSION MANUAL™

How to convert Volkswagen
BUS
or VAN
to CAMPER

Lindsay Porter

Applies to all VW Transporter T3/T25 & T4 Panel Vans & People Carriers (not Pick-up or Crew cab) 1980 to 2003

Have a great time converting your VW van to a Camper - and save a fortune! With 800 colour illustrations, this manual guides you every step of the way.

ISBN: 978-1-903706-45-9
Paperback • 27x20.7cm • 224 pages

Index